Ginsburg, H. Louis

The Israelian Heritage of Judaism

TEXTS and STUDIES

OF

THE JEWISH THEOLOGICAL SEMINARY
OF AMERICA

VOL. XXIV

THE
ISRAELIAN HERITAGE
OF JUDAISM

THE STROOCK PUBLICATION FUND

Established in Memory of Sol M. and Hilda W. Stroock and
Robert L. Stroock

THE
ISRAELIAN HERITAGE
OF JUDAISM

by

H. LOUIS GINSBERG

SABATO MORAIS PROFESSOR EMERITUS OF BIBLE

The Jewish Theological Seminary of America

NEW YORK
THE JEWISH THEOLOGICAL SEMINARY OF AMERICA
5742 – 1982

Library of Congress Cataloging in Publication Data

Ginsberg, Harold Louis.
   The Israelian heritage of Judaism.

   (Texts and studies of the Jewish Theological
Seminary of America ; v. 24)
   Includes bibliographical references and index.
     1. D document (Biblical criticism) 2. Bible.
O.T.—Theology. I. Title. II. Series.
BS1181.17.G56 1982   221.6   82-8924
ISBN 0-87334-013-2   AACR2

MANUFACTURED IN THE UNITED STATES OF AMERICA

TABLE OF CONTENTS

Preface

As this monograph goes to press, it is my pleasant duty to express appreciation of what it owes to Professor Gerson D. Cohen, Chancellor of The Jewish Theological Seminary of America, for accepting it for inclusion in the Seminary's series *Texts and Studies*; to Mrs. Harriet Catlin, the Seminary's Director of Special Projects, for the skillful management of its production; to my former students Rabbi Benjamin E. Scolnic and Mrs. Lorraine Sherman, the one for help in the technical editing and proofreading of a section of the work, the other for drafting the Index of Bible Passages; and to Mr. Bernard Scharfstein and the staff of Ktav Publishing House, for courteous and efficient service.

Above all, I give thanks to Him who gives strength to the weary.

H. L. Ginsberg

New York, Sivan 5742 — June 1982

THE ISRAELIAN HERITAGE OF JUDAISM

Preliminary: The Term Israelian

The word *Israelian* is not listed in any of the dictionaries I have in my study. An example of the purposes for which I coined it is the characterization, in a single word, of the eighth century B.C.E. prophet Deutero-Hosea (the prophet of Hosea 4–14, properly *"Deutero-*Hosea") in contrast to his younger contemporary Isaiah. "Israelite" would not do, since in other than the political sense "Israel" embraced the southern kingdom (i.e. Judah, or the House of Judah) as well as the northern. On this Isaiah and Hosea are in perfect agreement. For Isaiah, who prophesies concerning *Judah and Jerusalem* in the name of "YHWH of Hosts, the Mighty One of *Israel"* (Isa 1:24), has recourse to the awkward phrase "the *two Houses* of Israel" in the remarkable verse (Isa 8:14) "He (i.e. YHWH of Hosts, v. 13) shall be for his holy domain (move back the *w* at the beginning of *wl'bn* to the end of the preceding word, cf. Ps 114:2) a stone to strike against: a rock to stumble against for the *two Houses of Israel* etc." And Deutero-Hosea for his part designates the *two* kingdoms as "the tribes (i.e. the two political divisions) of *Israel"* (Hos 5:9).[1]

"(The) Israelians" would, therefore, be a good rendering of *bne yiśra'el* in Hos 2:1–2 — especially in 2:2, where it is explicitly coordinated with *bne yhuda* — and in II Chr. 13:12, where an antithesis to the Judites is implied. Such an antithesis is also implied in Amos 2:11; 3:1; 9:7; for this Judite prophet, struck by the constant harp-

---

[1] Cf. the annotated renderings of Isa 8:11–16 and Hos 5:8–13 on pp. 367 and 773 of *The Prophets (Nevi'im) — A new translation of the Holy Scriptures, Second Section* (Jewish Publication Society of America), Philadelphia 1978.

ing by his hosts on elements of salvation history which were little stressed in his homeland, is at pains to impress upon them that those acts of grace do not in any case warrant their sense of impunity. In general, Amos is a veritable mine of information on Israelian beliefs and practices in the first half of the eighth century B.C.E.

I. THE EMERGENCE OF JUDAISM

Less immediately obvious than the usefulness of a preliminary discussion of the term "Israelian" is the need for a discussion of the term "Judaism." Judaism is clearly an outgrowth of Judite Yahwism, and just where it is best to draw the line beween "post-exilic Yahwism" and Judaism may seem at first sight unduly hard to determine and of little practical importance. Nevertheless, there are certain advantages to regarding Judaism as having crystallized ca. 410 B.C.E. 1. *In the eastern Diaspora,* this date lies on the hither side of the progressive Hebraization of the personal names to which the Murashu's Sons documents bear witness[2] as also of the missions of Ezra and Nehemiah to Judah. 2. *In Egypt,* it lies on this side of the observance of the week of unleavened bread in 419 B.C.E.[3] and the writing of the two undated ostraca alluding to the pascal sacrifice[4] and to the sabbath[5] respectively. 3. *In Judah,*

---

[2] See most recently E.J. Bickerman, *PAAJR* 45 (1978), 1–28.

[3] See my revised treatment of "the Passover papyrus" in *ANET*[3] (1969), p. 491.

[4] See E.L. Sukenik and E.Y. Kutscher, *Kedem* 1 (1942), 53–56.

[5] It has most recently been republished by J.H. Tigay in *Enṣiqlopedia Miqra'it* 7 (1976), pp. 515–6, where a photograph of the original is reproduced from A. Dupont-Sommer, *Semitica* 2 (1949), p. 30, and the transcription into modern Hebrew printed characters follows that of F. Rosenthal, *An Aramaic Handbook* I/1, Wiesbaden 1967, pp. 12–13, into Latin characters. It is disappointing to find that neither Rosenthal (*op. cit.* I/2, p. 116 (s,v. *l'*) nor Tigay in his Hebrew rendering (*loc. cit.*) has noted that *hn l'* (ll. 3,7), following directly on *hylyhh* ("by Yhh!"), corresponds exactly to the Hebrew *'im lo* (to be translated, *if translated at all,* "Surely") with which *affirmative oaths* (or asseverations) are introduced in II Sam 19:14, II Ki 9:26; Isa 5:9; 14:24 (though the *negative oaths* [or negations] introduced by *'im* without *lo* are far more numerous; e.g. Num 13:21–23 [cf. Ps 95:11]; I Sam 14:45; II Sam 14:19b; I Ki 17:1,12; II Ki 2:2, 4, 6, etc.). Which makes it all the more gratifying to be able to note that our ostracon's *hn l'* is cited, along with other pertinent comparative material, apropos of the Hebrew negative/asseverative *'im/'im lo* by Baumgartner-Hartmann-Kutscher, *Hebräisches und aramäisches Lexikon zum AT,* Lieferung I (1967), pp. 58b–59a. (Of course, much in the ostracon still remains to be elucidated.)

finally, the year 410 B.C.E. comes (a) after the activity of Nehemiah and its motivations as reflected in what may, with reasonable safety, be identified as extracts from his own account of his governorship, as well as (b) either after or during the labors of the main compiler of Ezra-Nehemiah, who created an ethno-"historical" hypothesis and a halakic midrash to serve as theoretical underpinning for the situation and the attitudes that had come to prevail in Judah as a result of Nehemiah's governorship. At the same time, both Nehemiah, by his diction when he wants to sound "biblical" (i.e. when praying, as in Neh. 1:5 ff., or when adjuring a group of delinquent citizens of his bailiwick, 13:25b), and our compiler, by his choice of texts to employ as pretexts for halakic midrash, illustrate the important role played in Judaism by what may be its most important piece of Israelian heritage: Deuteronomy.

In the preceding paragraph, the last sentence but one implies, of course, that a great deal of the material which follows the caption "Matters relating to Nehemiah son of Hachaliah" (Neh 1:1) does not derive from Nehemiah's own account of his governorship, even if it be granted (though even that is by no means certain) that the independent documents 3:1–32 and 7:6 ff. (with the connecting half-verse 7:5b) and the connecting narrative 11:1–2 were incorporated into the account by Nehemiah himself. For in any case chs. 8–10 are not by him, and neither are 11:3—13:3 (though individual verses in the story about the happy Levite-led celebration of the inauguration of the walls of Jerusalem [12:27 ff.]—which is so reminiscent of the happy Levite-led ceremonies of the Chronicler [I Chr 15:16–25; II Chr 20:27–30; 29:30; 30:21–27]—may be freely adapted from an otherwise lost portion of Nehemiah's narrative). Further, 13:6 (with its egregious "Artaxerxes king of Babylon") is not by Nehemiah.

One of the several studies by G. Kh. Sarkisian which supplement

---

[5a] In this prayer, Nehemiah echoes, in that order, phrases from Deut 10:17; 7:8,11; 4:27 (28:64); 30:3–4; 12:11.

this limited biblical material with data from external sources is his paper "City Land in Seleucid Babylonia."[6] It treats of the (walled) cities of Babylonia, which had enjoyed a privileged status and a measure of self-government since at least Sargonid times (8th–7th centuries B.C.E.), and it shows that they controlled considerable land in their neighborhoods.[6a] Chancellor G.D. Cohen, who brought Sarkisian's articles to my attention, opined that Nehemiah took those "city states" as his model; hence his resolve to fortify Jerusalem and his emphatic declaration to Sanballat, the governor of Samaria, and his colleagues that they could never have any "share, right, or remembrance" in Jerusalem (Neh 2:20). Internally, Nehemiah recognized those nobles and councilors (ḥorim and sganim)—no doubt landowners—who resided in Jerusalem as some sort of consultative body. They are among those to whom he reveals his plan of fortifying Jerusalem and whose approval for it he receives (2:16–18); they are at the head of those he encourages in the face of the reports that have been received of an impending attack by hostile neighbors on the men engaged in the work of fortification (4; 1–8), and they are at the head of those he instructs to be ready to rally at the spot where a ram's horn is sounded (4:13). But the most famous occasion of all was when, on learning of the wretched plight of the poor, including the poor peasants, he

---

[6] *Vestnik Drevnej Istorii*, 1953, No. 1, pp. 59–73—republished in an English translation in *Ancient Mesopotamia, Socio-Economic History, A Collection of Studies by Soviet Scholars*, Moscow 1969, pp. 312–331. See further Sarkisian, *VDI* 1952, No. 1 (39/1) pp. 68–85; *VDI* 1955, No.4 (54), pp. 136–159.

[6a] Surely such apparent "city states" or "temple states" were the models that influenced Ezekiel to speak in ch. 16 as if Jerusalem constituted the whole of Israel in the wider sense and in ch. 23 as if Oholah-Samaria constituted the whole of Israel in the narrower sense and Oholibah-Jerusalem the whole of Judah. But that the late post-Isaian passages Isa 4:3; 10:24; 30:19 speak of Jerusalem-Zion in this manner is no doubt due to the "city-state" features of late Persian Judah, which had apparently been enhanced in Nehemiah's time by the migration to Jerusalem of one-tenth of the inhabitants of the "settlements" (*'arim*) where surely at least some of them retained some property, including farm land—Neh 11:1). Particularly revealing is the contrast between the first of those post-Isaian passages and the genuine Isaian verse 6:13, which says with reference to *the land* (see the end of 6:12) that what survives of its population shall be a holy strain.

convened a great assembly at which he exhorted the nobles and councilors, in the name of the fear of God (5:9), to cancel the debts owed to them, himself setting the example along with his kinsmen and attendants (who had likewise lent money and grain). Those present agreed, and he reinforced their promise with a priestly adjuration and a curse (5:12-13). To be sure, Morton Smith has diagnosed Nehemiah as a "tyrant" similar to those who, earlier in the fifth century, had made themselves absolute rulers of the Persian provinces along the Aegean Sea, and has characterized the foregoing debt cancellation action as demagogy—designed to gain the support of the poor peasants against the "gentry"—of a piece with the demagogic tricks by which some of the tyrants achieved absolute control.[7] However, Nehemiah himself also remitted the debts owed to him; and since he induced the "gentry" to comply by appealing to their piety, and since in subsequent crises we find him utilizing not any help from the peasantry but solely his own powers as governor and his own determination 13:4-9, 19-20, 25-29), the tyrant hypothesis seems to be superfluous. Nehemiah again gives "fear of God" and a desire to lighten the burden of "this people" as his reasons for making no use of his right to "the governor's bread allowance" (5:14-19) despite the expense of keeping up a table to which he invited not only visitors from among the nations but the Jerusalem gentry, whose number had increased, no doubt as a result of the migration to it of one-tenth of the population of Judah (11:1-2), to 150 (did he really play host to all of them daily?). He was intensely pious, and his idea was evidently to make all of Judah live as nearly as he was able to in conformity with the will of God.

The closing of the breaches in Jerusalem's wall and the furnishing of its entrances with gates were not intended to make it safe from attacks by any serious military force (cf. Neh 3:35) but (apart from satisfying the requirement for a "city state") to foster a sense

---

[7] M. Smith, *Palestinian Parties and Politics that Shaped the Old Testament*, New York and London 1971, pp. 126-147, 252-262. But unlike the Greek governors of Persian provinces, Nehemiah did not aspire to independence, ibid. bottom third of p. 136.

of cohesiveness and exclusiveness in the temple community. Nehemiah also took advantage of those gates to lock out of the city on the sabbath would-be vendors of provisions, Neh 13:19–21. Note well that while the purveyors of fish from the coast (which was no part of Nehemiah's bailiwick) are referred to in v. 16 as Tyrians, there is obviously no question about the unimpeachable Israelite identity of the sabbath-breaking farmers of 13:15, and that while Nehemiah chides the Jerusalem gentry for not having put a stop to this traffic themselves[8] he evidently saw no possibility of enforcing sabbath observance in the open country by one swift campaign.

Then how about his brutal procedure against those who had married Ashdodite women[9] (13:23–27)? There is not the slightest hint that such wives were more lax in Israelite observance than the Judite ones and, to judge by modern analogies, some of them may even have been stricter. Anyway, the only alarming consequence of such matches that Nehemiah mentions is that some of the children born of them spoke Ashdodite instead of Judean.[9a] That was clearly a threat to the cohesiveness of the temple community, and Nehemiah tells us that he had some men flogged[10] and made them

[8] One wishes one could date exactly Jer 17:19 ff. As Jeremian, of course, vv. 19–20 are particularly delightful: Jeremiah addresses the "kings" (pl.) of Judah who are entering and leaving "by all these gates" of Jerusalem.

[9] The last two words in v. 23 ('ammoniyyot mo'ăbiyyot) look suspiciously like additions owing to the absence of the conjunction w before either of them, and the last three words of v. 24 are if anything even more suspicious because of their impossible position (instead of following directly on 'ašdodit). Apart from that, the province of Ashdod had a long common border with the most thickly settled part of Judah, whereas Ammon had only a short one with a less populous part of Judah, and Moab had none. I find it all but impossible to believe that the passage originally spoke of any but Ashdodite spouses.

[9a] It is hardly necessary today to emphasize that these were not simply two dialects of Aramaic but that Judean was (a later form of) the same language that is so designated in II Ki 18:6, 28//Isa 37:11, 13 while Ashdodite was probably a variety of Phoenician. (In the Philistine masculine personal name 'bd'l'b, of the eighth century B.C.E., the theophoric element 'l'b recalls the Ugaritic word ilib, which seems to mean something like "deified ancestor.") An interesting feature of Nehemiah's Judean speech will be discussed at the end of Chapter VII.

[10] The next word, in view of Isa 50:6 (cf. Ezek 29:18), may mean "I slapped, or bruised, them" rather than "I plucked them" (otherwise, why "them," instead of "their hair" or "their beards" in agreement with Ezra 9:3?).

(or their neighbors?) swear to desist from the practice. And very interesting are the following two circumstances: 1. Though he hurls at them Deut 7:3 recast as an adjuration, he inveighs against "foreign wives" without qualification, even though Deut 7:3 itself refers only to the seven aboriginal peoples of Deut 7:1, and even though all of Ezra-Nehemiah apart from Nehemiah's memoirs adds "of the peoples of the land" in order (as we shall see) to imply that the contemporary non-Israelites of the Holy Land are subject to the same exclusion as those of Moses' time. 2. Nehemiah's point is not that Ashdodite wives are forbidden by the Torah (this word does not occur in his memoirs) but that even Solomon lapsed into sin owing to "the foreign wives."

Similarly Nehemiah quotes no Scripture in reporting that he exiled (? lit. "drove him from my presence") a grandson of the high priest, who married a daughter of Sanballat, though he does employ the phrase "the contamination of the priesthood and the covenant of the priesthood and the Levites" (13:28-29). Of course, in light of 2:19 ff.; 3:33 ff.; 4:1-2; 6:1-8, 10 ff., that marriage was an act of treason against Nehemiah and his temple state. Perhaps most puzzling of all is Nehemiah's failure to invoke the specific prohibition of Deut 23:4, 6 against admitting Ammonites and Moabites into the YHWH community — or even seeking their friendship — in the matters of Tobiah, "the Ammonite minister (*'ébed*)" scil. of Sanballat (2:10, 19), and the action he took to evict him from the chamber in the temple court which the priest Eliashib had allotted to him, 13:4-5, 7-9. It would seem that Nehemiah, though pious, was but an indifferent Bible scholar.

This judgment need not be reversed even if it is assumed (without prejudice) that the signatures of Nehemiah and Zedekiah (Rudolph wonders if the latter may have been Nehemiah's secretary) to the covenant of Neh 10 are genuine; for in any case it was not drafted by him, though it perhaps does not contain anything that he would have objected to. This no doubt includes the strict distinction between "the peoples of the *land*" (vv. 31, 32) and "the peoples of the *lands*" (v. 29). Just as in the preceding confession (ch.

9), the former (9:24) means the peoples of the Promised Land and the latter (9:39) *the peoples of other lands,* so in 10:31 and 32 the former are the peoples of Palestine outside Judah, whom the covenanters covenant not to intermarry with and not to buy supplies from on sabbaths and holy days; but "the peoples of the *lands*" (10:29) are those of Babylonia and adjoining regions which a section of the covenanters had avowedly themselves belonged to originally but had forsaken in order to embrace the teaching (*Torah*) of God. After all, if Nehemiah had indeed studied the list of earliest repatriates which we have in Neh 7:6 ff., then he knew that they included the group named in vv. 61-62, of some 642 souls, who were unable to say whether or not they were of Israelite descent but whom there never was any question of expelling from the community or subjecting to any disabilities.

And as a matter of fact, even "the main compiler of Ezra-Nehemiah," who takes an uncompromising attitude concerning "the peoples of the *land,*" and attributes to Ezra the actual expulsion of wives recruited from them together with the half-Israelite children they had borne, and on explicit scriptural grounds, is just as far removed as Neh 10 from any desire to exclude converts from among "the peoples of the *lands.*" For one thing, he includes in his compilation Ezra 2, a duplicate of the same "list of repatriates" we encountered above in Nehemiah 7, with the same paragraph on families which were not able to say whether or not they were of Israelite stock (and in fact the number of such persons is here [Ezra 2:60] 652 instead of the mere 642 in the corresponding verse in Nehemiah 2); and the evidence is much more complete than that.

Our friend, who planned this compilation as a continuation of Chronicles, actually began his work at the end of Chronicles. II Chr 36:22-23 must have been added by him because (1) it is identical with Ezra 1:1-3 down to *wyá'al,* and (2) the sense is incomplete without the end of 1:3. Where shall the subject "go up" to, and what shall he do there, and what has his mere "going up" anywhere to do with the command of YHWH to *Cyrus to build a temple for him in Jerusalem which is in Judah?* Only Ezra 1:3 after *wyá'al*

tells us that. In fact, it doesn't really become clear what Cyrus himself proposes to contribute to the building of the temple until we
read v. 4, which implies permission (though not more than that!)
to the people who remain behind in the settlements from which the
"halutzim" set out for Jerusalem to contribute to the latter's
equipment and also to send through them free will contributions
to the temple itself.[10a] And we don't learn of any direct contribution of Cyrus's own until we come to Ezra 1:7-8.[11]

But it is not only II Chron 36:22 ff. that was added at the end of
Chronicles by our friend "the main compiler of Ezra-Nehemiah."
In my opinion, there can be no question but it was he who in v. 21
added clauses a*b*-b*a*—"until the land should make up for[12] its
(unkept) years of rest by resting through the entire period of its
desolation." For while it is correct that Jeremiah (who has already

---

[10a] To date, I have found no reason to modify my old interpretation of this verse, JBL 79
(1960), 167–69.

[11] I don't think anybody has seriously questioned the historicity of this action of Cyrus.
Anyone who is inclined to do so had better first scrutinize the rendering of Isa 52:11, with
the footnote to it, in *The Prophets/Nevi'im*, Jewish Publication Society, Philadelphia 1978, p.
476. For the reader's convenience, I reproduce them here:

> Turn, turn away, touch naught unclean
> As you depart from there;
> Keep pure, as you go forth from there,
> You who bear the vessels of the Lord.*

*Cf. Ezra 1:7–8; 5:14–15.

What *can* this be but an apostrophe to those who are conveying back to Jerusalem the vessels
of its old temple which have been released by Cyrus? (Cf. also Isa 52:12.) In the famous
Cyrus Cylinder (ANET³ 1969, p. 326a bottom–326b top), we find named certain "sacred
cities on the other side of the Tigris" whose inhabitants had been displaced and whose
temples had long lain in ruins, their god-images having been carried off, and learn that
Cyrus righted those wrongs. How any important personage in his administration (hardly he
himself directly) may have learned about the similar wrongs that his Chaldean predecessors
had perpetrated in the sacred city of Jerusalem far beyond the Euphrates (from whose
temple, however, they had carried off not images, of which it had none, but precious vessels)
and may have been persuaded that Cyrus's piety required that similar restitution be made
there, is something about which we can only speculate. Perhaps some favorably placed
member of the upper class of the exiles from Judah took care of that.

[12] Though it is not necessary for the sense, I suggest that *raṣta* be emended to *tirṣe* or *rṣot*
for the sake of correct grammar.

been mentioned in v. 12) predicted that the Babylonian domination would last 70 years (Jer. 25:11–12; 29:10), he never predicted that the land would be desolate for 70 years, let alone stated that the purpose of the desolation was to atone for its unkept sabbath years. Our two clauses were clearly inspired by Lev 26:34–35, cf. v. 43. But this compels us to ask another question: What was our friend's purpose in interpolating those two clauses here? Did he, perchance, wish to imply that at least in the case of Judah the threat that the land would be totally deserted was fulfilled literally, so that it was not inhabited by a single soul until it was resettled by immigrants from Babylonia? Of course, only an interpolator would fail to realize that v. 20 couldn't very well be speaking about the whole land, since vv. 17–19 speak only of Jerusalem, but does anyone still doubt that the author of v. 21 a*b-ba was* an interpolator? But if this interpolator, as I claim, is "the main compiler of Ezra-Nehemiah," does it not behoove me to demonstrate that the latter holds that Judah, until colonized by repatriates from Babylonia, was a vacuum? Fair enough, but first let us see whether Lev 26 contains anything that might seem to lend color to the view that the fate of Judah differed, in this regard, from that of the erstwhile northern kingdom. It does: Lev 26:32b implies that at least a part of "the land" will not remain a vacuum but will be occupied by "your enemies"! Now we can turn to the story of our "main compiler etc."

His text of Cyrus's edict is followed by the sentence Ezra 1:5, "Thereupon the heads of the families of *Judah and Benjamin and the priests and the Levites,* that is, everyone whose spirit God roused, got ready to go up and rebuild the temple of YHWH in Jerusalem," in which the emphasis on the italicized expression is of course supplied by me—obviously because I regard it as of cardinal significance. First of all, what is its origin? Its origin is the first 12 verses of II Chron 11. These verses summarize the view of all the rest of II Chronicles on the ethnic makeup of the post-Solomonic kingdom of Judah, as is confirmed by constant recurrences of the dichotomy Judah and Benjamin, namely, in II Chr 14:7; 15:2, 8,

9; 17:14–16 (the astronomic army of Judah), 17–19 (the astronomic contingent of Benjamin); 25:8; 31:1; 34:9 end. Note how, with a fine disregard of geography (including the data in I Chr 4:24–43, if the author of II Chr 11 ff. knew that passage), even the tribe of Simeon is counted not to the residual kingdom of the Davidids but to the schismatic post-Solomonic kingdom of Israel (15:9; 34:6).[13]

Now, in II Chronicles itself it is occasionally implied that the tribes other than Judah and Benjamin (to which even Shemaiah is made to refer as brothers of Judah and Benjamin, II Chr 11:4) are always welcome to come and worship YHWH at Jerusalem, and it is related with obvious satisfaction that some of them sometimes did so and even settled permanently within the shrunken Davidic realm (II Chr 11:16 [and 17?]; 30:11; 31:1,6; 34:9,33). But as for our compiler of Ezra-Nehemiah, one may speculate, if one wishes, that he may have believed that by the time when Judah and Benjamin went into exile—and left behind in Judah a complete vacuum!—all the members of the other authentic tribes of Israel either had been carried off by the Assyrians and disappeared or had migrated to Judah and Benjamin and been absorbed by them. But whether or not he tried to reconcile his position with that of the Chronicler, the fact is that the next time he employs the phrase

---

[13] The passage II Chr 11:1–4 also occurs in the I Ki account of Rehoboam, namely as I Ki 12:21–24. But that is the last we ever hear in Kings either of a dichotomy Judah-Benjamin or, for that matter, of a prophet Shemaiah, whereas, as we have seen, the dichotomy Judah-Benjamin is continued right through II Chronicles, while Shemaiah recurs there until as far down as could reasonably be expected: II Chr 12:5, 15. Add to this that I Ki 12:21 glaringly contradicts the immediately preceding half-verse (I Ki 12:20b), and the obvious conclusion is that the erratic block I Ki 12:21–24, which fits organically into II Chr, was secondarily added to I Ki from Chronicles. There is an excellent analogy to this phenomenon: I Ki 8:4 from "and the tent of meeting" on is a startling erratic block in Kings; but it is simply reproduced from the corresponding part of II Chr 5:5, which is organic in Chronicles: see I Chr 16:39–42; 21:29–30; II Chr 1:3, 5, 13. Perhaps it was indeed already Rehoboam who managed to convert most of the Benjamite watershed (not including Bethel, however) into a buffer for his residence in Jerusalem; but if so, it must have been thanks to the Egyptian pharaoh Shishak, who temporarily captured from Jeroboam both Shechem and Penuel (the latter is in Transjordan); see B. Mazar, VT Suppl. 4 (1957), 57–66. Noth's emendation of *Judah* in I Ki 12:20 to *Benjamin* was never anything but an act of desperate arbitrariness.

"Judah and Benjamin" it is in the combination *"the adversaries* of Judah and Benjamin," Ezra 4:1, by which he characterizes "the population of the land" in its relation to "the population of Judah," 4:4—*now that the latter has one,* consisting of "the members of the exile community" (the phrase which here alternates, and is everywhere completely synonymous, with "Judah and Benjamin," 4:1).[14] How seriously our compiler means this can be seen from the

[14] M. Smith, *op.cit.,* (see n.7) pp. 104, 112 ff. and some of the pertinent notes at the back of that volume, unfortunately wallows in a morass of errors and misunderstandings mainly as a result of a wrong exegesis of Ezr 4:1. In the first place, he keeps rendering the phrase which I have translated "the *adversaries* of Judah and Benjamin" by the indefensible "the rivals of J. and B."; and in the second place, he wholly misses the significance of the equation "Judah and Benjamin" = "the members of the exile community." To begin with, the *masculine ṣar* can no more mean a mere "rival" than its Aramaic etymon *'ār.* The latter, as can be seen from Dan 4:16 end, is a synonym of *śānē* 'enemy,' and one has only to look up a Hebrew lexicon to see that the same is true—literally—of the Hebrew *ṣar.* Therefore "the *ṣarim* of J. and B." means the same thing as "your *'oybim* who dwell in it," which our "compiler of Ezra-Nehemiah," as explained at the beginning of our discussion of him, understood to refer to "your land" *outside Judah,* so that "the population of the land" who, In Ezra 4:4, thwart the building plans of "the (newly repatriated) *population of Judah"* can only refer to "your enemies" who dwell *outside Judah.* The origin of Smith's mistranslation "rivals" is evidently the conventional rendering of the *feminine ṣara* in I Sam 1:6, where an unambiguous rendering would be "co-wife." That, as can be seen in C. Brockelmann, *Lexicon Syriacum,*[2] p. 544b bottom, is also the meaning of *'arrtā,* the Syriac etymon of *ṣara,* and of its Arabic and Akkadian etyma. (Brockelmann obviously had difficulty in finding an appropriate Latin equivalent because, since Roman law did not recognize more than one legitimate wife, he could think of nothing nearer than *pellex* [usually spelled *paelex*], which can mean the rival of a legitimate wife but not a woman who is herself a legitimate wife of the same husband. Perhaps he would have done well to *coin* such a Latin word as *conuxor* and add in parentheses an exact English, French, or German equivalent such as *co-wife, co-épouse,* or *Mitgattin.* Anyway, we now know what *ṣara* means—and what *ṣar* does not.) In Haggai 2:4 and Zech 7:5, of course, which date from before the birth of the "Judah and Benjamin-exile community" fiction, "the people of the land" are nothing different from what they are in say, Jer 34:19, namely the (free) population *of Judah* as a whole, who are ethnically in no way different from Haggai, Zechariah, or Jeremiah, and are *not* to be confused with "the population of the land" in Ezr 4:4 who are specifically *non*-Judite and whose syncretism, if any, is therefore irrelevant to the question of syncretism in any element in Judah. That Smith's evidence for it is in any case (unlike that of Isa 57:5-13a; 65:3-7, 11; 66:3, 17) of a piece with the emperor's new clothes in Hans Christian Andersen's story is sensed by Smith himself (p. 112 bottom). Just what he means by saying (p. 113 top) that "Ezra reports" Ezra 4:1 ff. and by attributing to "Ezra" Ezra 3:13—4:1 (ibid., 11. ll-10 from below) I can only wonder, since these passages do not even claim to stem from Ezra. (Neither do they imply that the adversaries—not rivals!—lived "within earshot of the temple" site.) [Surely M. Smith will not deny that it is the non-Judites named in Neh 4:1-2 that are referred to as "our Ṣarim" in v. 5 and as "our *'oybim"* in v. 9.]

fact that, although he never uses the phrase Judah and Benjamin again except in 10:9, he repeats *(the members of) the exile community* in 6:16, 19, 20 (8:25 doesn't count because it refers to Ezra's group, which has just arrived); 9:4 (Ezra allegedly narrating, and with reference to those who arrived half a century earlier!); 10:6, 7, 8, 16. That the man who had the imagination to conceive such a bold theory should also prove to be a more lively narrator than the pedestrian one, or ones, of Chronicles is, after all, not surprising. That Zerubbabel and Jeshua laid the foundations of the new temple in 537 (3:8, 10–11) is hardly likely; for according to Haggai 2:18, they only did so in 520, and though Ezra 6:16 has "the Judean elders" (see vv. 6, 9)—Zerubbabel and Jeshua figure by name only in the introduction to this chapter—inform Tattenai that the foundations were laid back in the reign of Cyrus, it has them attribute this act to Sheshbazzar. Nevertheless, the narrator (in ch. 3) displays such a feeling for psychology that, after telling us (as the Chronicler would have) that Zerubbabel and Jeshua's laying of the foundations was the occasion for a Levite-led mass rejoicing, he adds the fine psychological touch that some of the older dignitaries, who had seen the old temple when it was still standing, were so overcome with emotion by the ceremony of the laying of the foundations for a new one that they wept. But that doesn't make a foundation-laying by those two men in the reign of Cyrus historically probable, and neither does their undeniable dramatic power make historical probabilities of the following scenes: Ezra's daylong public show of abject penitence, on his knees and with his garments rent and his palms spread out, because of "the sacrilege[15] of the exile community"; the effect of this spectacle on the pious among the spectators (9:3–10:8); the "shivering" of all the con-

---

[15] That is the usual meaning of the Hebrew word *má'al*, and the community's offense comes under this head because it consisted in the mingling of the holy stock with "the peoples of the land" (9:2; the emendation of *lands* to *land* will be justified further on). That is also why the penitent offender must, as in other cases of sacrilege, bring a penalty offering ('*ašam*, 10:19). See J. Milgrom, *Cult and Conscience*, Leiden 1976, 16–74.

vened men of Judah and Benjamin "over the gravity of the matter and with the winter cold"[16] (10:9); and the appointment of a committee which, in the space of ten days, prepared a list of some 110 transgressors (for nothing in the preceding account has implied that they were more than a tiny fraction of the total number of men in the province), all of whom dutifully expelled their alien wives together with the children they had borne.[17]

As regards the ethnic origin of those alien wives, Ezra 10:2 and 10:11 define it, in agreement with Neh 10:31, 32, as "from the peoples of the *land*"; and this, we argued above, differs significantly from the phrase "from the peoples of the *lands*," to which, according to Neh 10:29, a section of the covenanters themselves had belonged before embracing "the Teaching (*Torah*) of God." To those forbidden peoples, Ezra 9:1 applies eight names of which the first half—"Canaanites, Hittites, Perizzites, Jebusites"—are among those of the seven peoples which, according to Deut 7:1, the Israelites would encounter on invading the Promised Land and with whom they must not intermarry, while the other four—"Ammonites, Moabites, Egyptians, and Edomites (so read with I Esdras 8:66 for *Amorites*) '—figure in Deut 23:4 and 8 as names of neighboring peoples immigrants from which may either never or only with

---

[16] Lit. "rains"; but this plural is rightly interpreted by both I Esdras and II Esdras, and both in this verse and in v. 13, to imply not that it happened to be raining that day (in which case the author would surely have employed the singular *gésem*; cf. I Ki 18:41, 45) but that it was winter, in accordance with the usage of postbiblical Hebrew, in which *qáyiṣ* (summer) has been replaced by *ymot haḥamma* "the season of heat (lit. sun)" and *ḥórep* (winter) by *ymot haggšamim* "the season of cold (lit. rains)." In poetry, Song 2:4, even the singular *gésem* stands in synonymous parallelism with *staw* 'winter.' (*Šitā'*, the Arabic etymon of this last word, means 'rain' as well as 'winter.') Quite conceivably, the very choice of a date in the ninth month, Ezra 10:9—which is if anything the least severe of the winter months—may have been suggested by the scene described in Jer 36:22 of King Jehoiakim sitting, in the ninth month, in the winter palace with a fire burning on a brazier in front of him. That *gšamim* means "Winterzeit" was already seen by Frants Buhl (16th edition of Gesenius' lexicon) in 1915!

[17] The Hebrew of Ezra 10:14b is not very good; but whether or not one prefers to emend it in accordance with the corresponding clause in I Esdras (9:36) to "and they sent them away, both wives and children," it does *not* imply anything different from that.

restrictions be admitted into "the congregation of YHWH." Now, of course even the first four no longer inhabited any part of the Promised Land in postexilic times, while the other four never had. But this is a *midrash* which our compiler attributes to Ezra: namely, that *the present inhabitants of Samaria* are not only the enemies of Leviticus 26:32b but are *subject to the exclusion laws of Deut 7 and 23.*

But what is to be done about *'my h'rṣwt* in Ezra 9:1, 2? The same thing as was already done to it in v. 11 by J. Begrich, who prepared for *Biblia Hebraica*[3] Ezra 9:7–10:44 as well as all of Nehemiah and Chronicles. (Apparently H. H. Schaeder, who, to judge by the Prolegomena of editors Alt and Eissfeldt, had been assigned all of Ezra, was prevented by sickness or death from completing beyond Ezra 9:6.) When Begrich came to Ezra 9:11–12, he presumably realized that the author could not have intended to say that the land the Israelites were about to enter had been defiled by the peoples of Tibet and Patagonia and to make Israel's thriving in it dependent on its avoidance of connubium and friendship with those peoples, but only that it had been defiled by its own aborigines and that Israel must avoid mingling, or having any friendly relations with these. At any rate, he proposed emending *'my h'rṣwt* to *'my h'rṣ,* and if he had been asked to revise Ezra 1:1–9:6 as well, he would very likely have done the same in 3:3 and 9:1, 2. The slip was natural to an age which had a tendency to pluralize the recta of plural regentia, as can be seen from *gibbore ḥăyalim* (I Chr 7:5, 17); *śare haḥăyalim,* I Ki 15:20, is different, since each captain actually does command a "force" in its concrete sense of II Ki 18:17; Isa 36:2. As for *goye ha'áreṣ,* Ezra 6:21, it means "the nations of the *earth,*" as can be seen from the passages from which it is copied: Gen 18:18; 22:18; Deut 28:1. It therefore means the same thing as "the peoples of the lands," Neh 10:29, proselytes from which were always acceptable.

Such, then, are the "ethno-'historical' hypothesis" and the "halakic midrash" which, to employ the phraseology by which our compiler's labors are described at the beginning of this monograph, were "to serve as theoretical underpinning for the situation and the attitudes that had come to prevail in Judah as a result of Nehemiah's governorship."[18] That it is the thesis of the Book of Ezra that, whereas the fall of Samaria's kingdom was followed by a change in its ethnic character, the fall of the Davidic kingdom entailed for Judah only several decades of complete voidness of human occupation, after which the descendants of its original inhabitants were repatriated, was realized more than seventy years ago by Torrey.[18a] But according to him the purpose of this fiction was to enhance the prestige of the Jerusalem temple in the face of its rejection by the Samarians, whereas I have attempted, it is hoped successfully, to demonstrate that it was rather to justify the exclusion of non-Judeans—and Samarians in particular—from the community of the Jerusalem temple.

Before examining the records of Nehemiah and the work of this compiler for traces of Israelian heritage, let us consider another fifth-century figure whose exact date is uncertain: Malachi. Like Nehemiah, this prophet mentions the levitical tithes and the priest-

---

[18] It does not follow that the mission of Ezra is altogether unhistorical. The *substance* of the document Ezra 7:11-26 is not as improbable as is usually supposed. As regards v. 25, I pointed out long ago (*Eretz Israel* 9 [1969], 49a with nn. 13-16), that its sense is as follows: "And you, Ezra, in accordance with the wisdom you have from your God (or, the learning in the lore of your God that you possess), appoint as teachers (reading *spryn* with the LXX) and judges—for the purpose of judging all of his people (vocalizing the consonants of the Leningrad ms.—'*mh* [not '*m*']—as '*ammeh*, referring to 'your God' on the analogy of '*ammo* in 1:3) who reside in Transeuphrates—those who are versed in the laws of your God, and you and they (lit. 'you' *pl.*) shall instruct whoever is not." The document does not, therefore, confer on Ezra any authority over non-Jews.—Cf. also the word *šroši* '(corporal) punishment,' 7:26, whose form, meaning, and (Iranian) etymology were a mystery until the emergence, in the *Bodleian Aramaic Documents of the Fifth Century B.C.* published by G.R. Driver in 1954 and 1956, of the form *srwšyt'* (plural determined). It is therefore possible: (1) that Neh 8:1-12, though hardly pure history (even apart from the prolevitical interpolations and the addition of the name of Nehemiah at the beginning of v.9), does contain a grain of historical truth, namely, that public readings from the Torah date from this time; and (2) that Neh 8:13 ff. does reflect Ezra's role as a teacher of Torah. We shall see that the particular observance that is here enjoined is probably an Israelian element in Judah's heritage.

[18a] C.C. Torrey, *Ezra Studies*, 1910, reprinted by KTAV, New York 1970, pp. 153-5, 208 ff., 235-9, 262 ff., 321-3, referred to by Torrey, *The Second Isaiah*, Edinburgh 1928, p. 29, where he adds, "in opposition to the very dangerous pretensions of the community at Shechem and the temple on Mount Gerizim."

ly sacred gifts (Neh 13:5; Mal 3:8), of which at least the latter are enjoined only in the Priestly Code, Num 18:19 ff. But Nehemiah almost certainly knew them from practice rather than from the study of texts, since we have seen that the only Torah he reflects when he prays or wishes to speak quasi-biblically is Deuteronomy; and similary we are struck by the fact that Malachi speaks as if the priests traced their descent, in agreement with Deuteronomy, to Levi (Mal 2:1–9), not (with the Priestly Code) specifically to the Levite Aaron; and Mal 3:22 refers to the laws that God communicated to Moses at Horeb (so D), not at Sinai (so P). Evidently the Torah of the educated non-priest was Deuteronomy, which is not only suitable for popular study by reason of its parenetic (horatory) and non-technical style but which also enjoins study (Deut 6:6–9; 11: 18–20) and even public reading (Deut 31:9–13); and we have seen that our "compiler," who exhibits a knowledge not only of the Torah but also of the historical books of the Bible, makes passages in Deuteronomy (Deut 7:1–3; 23:4–8) the scriptural basis for the prohibition of intermarriage with Judah's neighbors.

II. The Israelian Origin of Deuteronomy

What makes all this significant is that Deuteronomy is a book of Israelian origin. This has been surmised before, and can now be proved conclusively. It can be shown that Deuteronomy is strongly influenced both in primary and in secondary passages by the diction of the Israelian Book of Hosea, that it also adopts Hosean[19] ideas, and that it even legislates measures in response to Hosean denunciations, whereas it borrows from Isaiah only diction and literary devices, and those only in secondary passages; and that conversely, only post-Isaian passages in the Book of Isaiah are indebted to Deuteronomy. If this is demonstrated, it will follow that Proto-Deuteronomy arose in a different area from Isaiah and before Isaiah had become a classic, in other words, in the kingdom of Israel between about 740 and about 725 B.C.E.

1. Deuteronomic echoes of Hosean diction

Deuteronomy	Hosea
$dgn \ldots tyrš \ldots yṣhr$, 7:13; 11:14; 12:17, etc.	2:10, 24
$ksp, zhb \ldots rby$, 8:13; 17:17	2:10
$t'kl$ $wšb't \ldots wrm$ $lbbk$, $wškḥt$ $'t$ $YHWH$ $'lhyk$	$'ny$ $yd'tyk$ (LXX $r'ytyk$) $bmbdr \ldots kmr'ytm$ $wyšb'w$,

---

[19] In the present context it is not necessary to distinguish between Hosea A (chs 1–3), going back to a prophet of the northern kingdom who prophesied in the early 860's B.C.E., and Hosea B (chs. 4–14), going back to a seer of the middle to late 740's, as I have argued in *Encyclopaedia Judaica* 8, cols. 1010 bottom ff.

hmwlykk bmbdr etc, 8:12–15   *šb'w wyrm lbm*

                                            'l kn škhwny, 13:5–6

br'b wbṣm' wb'yrm, 28:48   *'pšytnh 'rmh . . . whmtyh bṣm' . . .*

                                            wlqhty dgny . . . wtyrwšy . . .

                                            whṣlty ṣmry wpšty . . .

                                            2:5, 11[20]

2. Adoption of Hosean ideas by Deuteronomy

(a) The unique threat of punishment by return to Egypt in Deut 28:68 derives from Hosea 9:3a, 6,[21] in view of the demonstrated dependence of D in paragraph 1 above and in paragraphs 2b and 3 below.

(b) Deut 7:1–5, 12–26 is a fairly close parallel to Exod 23:20–33, except that it eliminates the role of YHWH's angel at the beginning of the Exodus passage. Citing my discovery[22] of a polemic against reliance on angels[23] in Hos 12, Weinfeld[24] has attributed Deut 7's suppression of the role of an angel in the prospective expulsion of the aborigines to the influence of Hos 12. (It cannot be due to the influence of Exod 34:11, since it will be shown further on that, on the contrary, Exod 34:11–13 is dependent on Deut 7:1–5.)

---

[20] It was Hannah Muller-Kodesh, *Bet Miqra* 42 (1970) 291, ll. 8–13, who pointed out that in Hosea the exceptional combination of all three privations (even paupers don't usually lack water, and the distress of siege or desert doesn't last long enough for a shortage of clothing to become a problem) is motivated by the need to disabuse the foolish woman of the notion that she owes all her commodities to her "lovers," 2:7b, whereas such motivation is lacking in Deuteronomy. Our verse, Deut 28:48, by the way, seems to be a secondary one, since the climax in vv. 45–46 sounds like an original conclusion.

[21] Muller-Kodesh, *ibid,* p. 290 with fn. 13.

[22] H. L. Ginsberg, *JBL* 80 (1961), 339–347. Cf. *The Prophets* (see above n. 1) on Hosea 12.

[23] Among other questionable assertions, Alexander Rofé, *Israelite Belief in Angels in the Pre-Exilic Period as Evidenced by Biblical Tradition,* Jerusalem, 1969 (mimeographed dissertation, Ivrit), attributes to me (with approval!) the view that Hosea opposes the *belief* in angels (p. 224, fn. 16), which is impossible in a man who recounts the tradition about Jacob's struggle with an angel as history. All I claimed was that the prophet denies that angels are of any importance, at least for Israel.

[24] M. Weinfeld, *Deuteronomy and the Deuteronomic School,* Oxford 1972, p. 14, n.5.

3. Deuteronomic legislation as, in part, response to Hosean prophecy

(a) The centralization of the cult which is required by Deut 12:8–18 is surely, at least in part, a response to the denunciation-cum-threat of Hos 8:11–14: "For Ephraim has multiplied altars—for guilt; his altars have redounded to his guilt: (12) The principles (?) of the instruction that I wrote for him have been treated as something alien. (13) They have *slaughtered* victims to no purpose (?)—only for *meat* to *eat*. YHWH has *not* been appeased by them. Behold, he will remember their iniquity and punish their sins: back to Egypt with them! (14) Since Israel has forgotten his Maker while building temples . . . I will send down fire on his cities and it shall devour his fortresses." The Deuteronomist evidently reasoned: if a multiplicity of altars and temples will lead to exile and devastation, the catastrophe may be averted by reducing the number of temples and altars to one, so that people may not rely on them as means for obtaining absolution. That this passage in Hosea was a factor in giving rise to the law in Deut 12, is confirmed by the recurrence in the latter of the phrase we have italicized in the former: *yzbḥw bśr wy'klw* (Hos 8:13) > *tzbḥ w'klt bśr* (Deut 12:15).

(b) Another Hosean denunciation-cum-threat that has surely been a factor in engendering Deuteronomic legislation is Hosea 10:13–15: (13) You have plowed wickedness; you have reaped iniquity; (and) you shall eat the fruits of treachery—all because you relied on your chariotry,[25] on your host of warriors. (14) But the din of war shall arise in[26] your own people, and all your walled cities shall be ravaged as Beth-arbel was ravaged by Shalman[27] on

[25] LXX (reflecting a Hebrew *brkbk*) for MT's *bdrkk*. Dahood's "power" won't do, because (aside from its colorlessness) *drk* "power" does not exist (any more than *drk* "assembly") either in Ugaritic or in Hebrew.

[26] Of a foreign invader, the author would have said "come up against (*'ala 'al*) your land." The prophet's point is that in a civil war, like the ones whose horrors Israel experienced as recently as in 747 B.C. (II Ki 15:10–22; Isa 9:17–20), chariotry and a standing force of infantry can only multiply Israel's own losses. [Isaiah knows in addition of the events of II Ki 15:23, 25.]

[27] Perhaps identical with the Shallum of II Kings 15:10 ff.; cf. the atrocities of Shallum's rival, *ibid.* v. 16.

a day of battle, when mothers and babes were dashed to death together. (15) . . . Israel's monarchy[28] shall utterly perish.[29]

We have just seen how, in the hope of averting the exile to Egypt and the destruction of the settlements in the homeland which Hos 8:11 ff. threatens as punishment for the sins which Israel was emboldened to commit by the availability of a multitude of sanctuaries (by sacrificing at which it believed it could obtain YHWH's favor), the Deuteronomist produced Deut 12:5 ff. which limits the number of sanctuaries to one for the whole country. Analogously, it is partly with the motive of averting the hideous civil war, ending in the collapse of the monarchy, which Hos 10:13–15 threatens as a punishment for the sins Israel was emboldened to commit by its chariotry and its professional infantry, that the Deuteronomist enacts laws designed to eliminate these appanages of monarchy. This can only be surmised in the case of the Deuteronomic pericope on the king, Deut 17:14–20, but is hard to escape in the one on mobilization for war, 20:1–9.

(a) In Deut 17:16–17 are listed three possessions (horses, women, silver-and-gold) which a king must limit, with reasons for only the first two restrictions; the reason for the third is apparently not given until v. 20. Now, only the reason for the middle restriction is tolerably clear at first sight: too many women are liable to turn the. king's heart away (from loyalty to YHWH), as can be seen from the example of Solomon, I Ki 11:4–8. In the case of the other two, the ostensible reason does not seem to be the real one. The admonition against acquiring many horses purports to be motivated by a desire to obviate the necessity of sending commercial representatives to Egypt (cf. I Ki 10:28), whither YHWH once declared that Israel should never return. But though this declaration is recalled again in 28:48, it is unknown outside Deuteronomy, and it may be derived midrashically from a tradition like that of Exod 14:13;

---

[28] So *mlk* is also to be rendered above, in v. 7.
[29] Because it is the monarchy that maintains chariotry and a standing army.

analogously, we shall see that D modifies the original tradition about the hour of the Exodus in Deut 16:1 end, 6 end. At least an additional purpose of the prohibition of acquiring many horses may well be to prevent the building of a combat force of chariotry; and similarly an unspoken motive for the prohibition of amassing gold and silver "to excess" (m'od) would seem to be that of placing the maintenance of a standing army beyond the king's reach.

(b) For the elimination of chariotry and professional soldiers is surely a basic assumption of Deut 20:1–9. Even the introductory sentence, beginning with the clauses "When you take the field against your enemies, and you see horses and chariots . . .," hints that Israel's defense force will lack this equipment. Then one has only to note the exemptions that the officials proclaim in vv. 5–8—presumably to a mass of men consisting of contingents from the various settlements which have rallied at a central point, with presumably every man bearing his own privately owned weapons, as in the days of the Judges. Professional soldiers may conceivably build houses, but hardly plant vineyards. Even less likely are professional soldiers, after receiving their allowances, in kind and in money, for a period of years, to be given the option of leaving for home just when an occasion for the use of their services arises. But above all, how can this option be offered to a professional soldier who claims to lack physical courage (v.8)? Surely, a man afflicted with this deficiency would hardly have chosen arms as his profession to begin with. And since the "comrades" of a professional soldier are necessarily likewise professionals, there is surely little danger of their being infected by the faintheartedness of one of their number—unless the authorities are so inept as to suggest the idea to them.

Of course Deuteronomy's legislation on the king and on war is unrealistic. A king who plays no part either in the administration of justice or in leadership in war, and who is content with the sole duty of having a scroll of the Deuteronomic Teaching copied for him by the Levitical priests and spending all his time studying it, will be either superseded or reduced to a mere figurehead by a man

who is ambitious to govern. But Josiah, who made Deuteronomy
the constitution of his realm, was more than a figurehead; and it is
significant that the centralization of the cult, which he pursued
vigorously, succeeded, whereas to dispense with mercenaries was
probably too impractical for him even to attempt.[30]

[30] To judge by the references to Kittites (either Cypriotes or men from the region of the
Aegean) in 10 ostraca from the seventh-century stratum of Arad, Y. Aharoni, *Ktwbwt 'rd*
(Hebrew), Jerusalem 1975, p. 163, col. b.

III. OTHER LITERATURE OF ISRAELIAN ORIGIN
—THE HEZEKIAN REFORMATION

(a) Micah C (Mi 6–7)

Before we take up the question how Israelian books like Hosea and Deuteronomy found their way into late preexilic Judah and how they affected its religion and culture, let us see what other biblical literature can be identified with any degree of probability as of Israelian provenience. Micah 6–7 — or Micah C — will prove a convenient starting point.[31] That its connection with Mi 1–5 is secondary is suggested, first of all, by the elaborate exordium Mi 6:1–2. As for the content, Micah 6:9–12 arraigns a "city" in terms that are curiously reminiscent of Amos's arraignment of Samaria, Amos 8:4–6, and the reproach "Yet you have kept the laws of Omri and all the practices of the House of Ahab" (Mi 6:16) becomes more pointed when it is conceived of as directed against Jeroboam II, a ruler of the very dynasty which supplanted that of Omri and Ahab. Indeed, the entire paragraph Mi 6:13–16 — a reproof to the listener for failing to be moved to repentance by previous chastisements, followed by a threat of worse to come — was apparently the less finished forerunner of Amos 4:6–12 that served Amos as a model.[32] But above all, the point in time at which our prophet is

---

[31] The reasons for marking off Mi 4–5, as Micah B, from both chs. 1–3 and chs. 6–7 will be given further on. It would be useful to look up all the passages referred to below in the English translation of The Jewish Publication Society's *The Prophets (Nevi'im)*, Philadelphia 1978, pp. 839 ff.

[32] I also have a feeling that our author's summing up of true religion by the three words *goodness (ḥésed), justice,* and *your God,* Mi 6:8, is echoed by Hosea 12:7. (Incidentally, *ḥésed* in lieu of *ṣédeq* or *ṣdaqa* is limited to these two passages and Ps 101:1, and in the last named passage *YHWH* as a third term is reminiscent of "your God" in the two prophetic ones. Is Ps 101 also of Israelian origin?

standing is indicated by 7:14. Since the only still unsatisfied wish for the restoration of Israel's territories is Bashan and Gilead, we are obviously in the early years of Jeroboam II, when Israel is in possession of all its old territories in Western Palestine thanks to the three victories of Jeroboam's father Joash over the Arameans, II Ki 13:25, but neither Joash nor, as yet, Jeroboam, has recovered Transjordan. Jeroboam accomplished this during the prophetic ministry of Amos, Amos 6:13 (the last years of Joash and/or the early years of Jeroboam had brought reverses, Amos 4:10): Lodebar (so read) was in Gilead, II Sam 15:27; Karnaim, in Bashan, Gen 14:5; I Macc 5:26, 43, 44.

Now that Israelian authorship of Mi 6–7 is assured, we may note that a feature which is characteristic of Israelian prophecy and psalmody in contrast to those of Judah is exceptionally prominent in Mi 6–7, and can be of help in identifying Israelian psalms. The feature in question is the stress on the earlier salvation history: the Exodus, the wilderness tradition, and the conquest. Our prophet, in addition to praying, 7:15, "Show us wondrous deeds as in the days when You sallied forth over the land of Egypt," cites the following list of "YHWH's acts of grace," drawn entirely from "the older salvation history": (Mi 6:4–5) "I brought you up from the land of Egypt, I redeemed you from the house of bondage,[33] and I sent Moses, Aaron, and Miriam to lead you.[34] (5) My people, remember what Balak king of Moab plotted against you, and how Balaam son of Beor responded to him. [Recall your passage][35] from Shittim to Gilgal—and you will know YHWH's acts of grace."

Now, the salvation history connected with the Exodus and the

---

[33] This epithet of Egypt occurs mainly in the E-D strand of literature: Exod 13:3; 20:2; Deut 5:6; 6:12: 7:8; 8:14; 13:6, 11 (Jud 6:8). Under the influence of, primarily, Deuteronomy, it occurs in seventh-century Judite prophecy at Jer 34:13.

[34] Note the fullness of detail. The only other passage outside the Pentateuch in which Miriam is named is I Chr 5:29. Ps 77: 21, expressing the same sentiment as our passage, names only Moses and Aaron.

[35] (Zkr) 'brk has apparently dropped out after the similar graph b'wr.

wilderness also plays an important part in the prophetic messages of the two fellow countrymen of the author of Mi 6–7 which make up the Book of Hosea:[36] Hos 2:17 [15]; 11:1; 12:10[9]; 13:4 (in the last passage, translate 'ever since [the land of] Egypt'); 12:14 [13]; ğ10; 13:5. It also bulks large in the message of Amos, a Judite sojourning in Israel[37] whose tone shows that he was reacting to the unwarranted assumption of impunity that his hosts based on traditions which in his homeland had drifted to the periphery of theological specualtion, Am 2:11; 3:1; 9:7.

But the situation in this regard is quite different in the eighth-century prophecy of Judah. There is not a single certainly Isaian reference to the exodus-wilderness tradition, and it is obvious that "the older salvation history" has at best been pushed to the periphery of his theology by the Zion and David ideology. For Isaiah's belief in YHWH's election of Zion, it is sufficient to recall Isa 8:18b, "YHWH of Hosts who dwells on Mount Zion," and the remarkable vision (Isa 6) in which he sees YHWH holding court in the Jerusalem temple (cf. the altar, v. 6).[38] And Zion is even the center of Isaiah's future world (2:2–4), in which all the nations have been converted to monotheism and live in permanent peace with each other. For the miraculously elevated Temple Mount, which has attracted them in the first place, is also the spot to which they come with their mutual disputes and at which these are decided by YHWH Himself through an oracle.[38a]

---

[36] See above, n. 19.

[37] We can hardly reconstruct in detail the circumstances that made this man of Tekoa (Am 1:1) deliver his message in the sister kingdom, but an important factor was doubtless the status of Judah as a mere appendage, even if an autonomous one, to Israel during the period between its humiliating defeat by the latter (II Ki 14:8–14)—which must have included the outright annexation of the Benjamite watershed by Israel—and the Judite counterstroke some forty years later (Hos 5:8–10); see *The Fourth Congress of Jewish Studies*, Vol. I, Jerusalem 1967, pp. 91–93.

[38] On this famous theophany see H. L. Ginsberg, *The Supernatural in the Prophets with special reference to Isaiah* (The Goldenson Lecture, 1978, Hebrew Union College, Cincinnati), pp. 20–22.

[38a] For an exposition of this passage, see *ibid.*, pp. 14–15.

As for Isaiah's belief in the election of the line of David, it is best documented by his pronouncements during the Arameo-Ephraimite attack on Judah (Isa 9:7 [6] ff. and 7:1—8:10,[38b] ca. 733 B.C.E.). Whereas 9:7 ff. is directed only against Ephraim (as Israel is frequently called at this time), 7:2 tells us of a fresh report that has reached Jerusalem and thrown it into a panic: Aram has joined forces with Ephraim. From v. 6 we learn further that the aim of the attackers is to replace Judah's legitimate king by one "the son of Tabeel." No doubt it is because the latter was not a Davidid that 7:2 tells us not just that King Ahaz and his subjects but that "the House of David" and its subjects were terror-stricken. The fact that the dynasty itself is threatened is surely the reason for Isaiah's unbridled fury both here and in ch. 9 and for his confidence that the aggressors will meet with disaster: YHWH himself, in Isaiah's conviction, is committed to the perpetuity of David's dynasty, whereas the aggressors are only men.[39]

There are also, within the initial mass Isa 1–33, which, as is well known, is the repository of genuine Isaian pieces (though it is by no means exclusively Isaian), three predictions of an ideal Davidic prince (9:1 ff.; 11:1 ff.; 16:1 ff., to which add 14:32, 30a) which are certainly Judite and all of which seem to contain a preexilic core; and one is tempted to trace specifically Isaiah's hand in verses like Isa 11:9 and 16:3–6 + 14:32, 30a.

    1. 11:9   (a) V. 9b is echoed by Habakkuk, who is still preexilic. Hab 2:13a, 14 ought probably to be placed after v. 20 and translated: "For behold, it has been decreed by YHWH of Hosts (namely, in Isa 11:9b) that all the earth must become as full of awareness of YHWH's grandeur as the sea is covered with water." Note that Habakkuk has here, in agreement with Hab 2:20 ("*hush* before him all the earth"), substituted the lesser "awareness of YHWH's grandeur" for Isaiah's "mindfulness of (i.e. obedience

---

[38b] Again it is advisable to follow the drift of these passages with the help of The Jewish Publication Society's *The Prophets.*

[39] See *The Supernatural in the Prophets* (cf. n. 38 above), pp. 4 ff.

to) YHWH," and on the other hand employs *ha'áreṣ* in the wider sense of "the earth" instead of, like Isaiah, in the narrower one of "the land" (cf. Isa 11:9a). (b) Isa 11:9a exhibits Isaian diction: with (i) "my holy mount" for YHWH's land, cf. 14:25 (vocalize *hari*, cf. Ps 78:54); (ii) the coupling of *hera'* with *hišḥit* is marvelously Isaian, cf. 1:4acd. (c) Above all, the implication of 11:9 is precisely that of the last clause in 6:13: its (i.e., as the context shows, the land's) firm-standing part shall be a holy strain.[40]

2. *16:3-6 + 14:32, 30a*. The Moabite fugitives, having fled— apparently before Jeroboam II of Israel (II Ki 14:25; Amos 6:14 end)[41] —are advised to send "from Sela in the wilderness to the mount of Fair Zion" (v. 1), the following message: "(3) Give advice, offer counsel. At high noon make your shadow like night: conceal the outcasts; betray not the fugitives. (4) Let Moab's outcasts find asylum in you; be a shelter for them against the despoiler."[42] For lawlessness[43] has vanished, . . . and marauders have perished from the land. (5) And a throne shall be established in goodness, in the tent of David, and on it shall sit in faithfulness a ruler devoted to justice and zealous for equity.[44] (14:32) But what will he answer the envoys of that nation? "Zion was established by

---

[40] So the clause is translated in *The Supernatural in the Prophets etc.* (see above note 38), p. 17, where the whole of Isa 6:9-13 is interpreted and the comparison with Isa 11:9 is made.

[41] W. Rudolph, *Hebrew and Semitic Studies Presented to G. R. Driver*, Oxford 1963, 130 ff.

[42] From here through 16:6 seems to be added by the prophet, implying: yes, Zion is an ideal place of asylum, but—

[43] Rd. with others *ḥmṣ*, a variant of *ḥms*, Ps 71:4.

[44] In JBL 69 (1950), 54 f., I proposed substituting for *mhr*, which is both abnormal in spelling (with no *y* after the *h*) and awkward in meaning (what is "an expert in righteousness"?) the reading *š(o)h(e)r*, which is a synonym of *doreš* and in fact stands in parallel to it in Prov 11:27 (as do the perfect consecutives of *drš* and *šhr* in Ps 78:34). Rudolph (see n. 41), p. 136, argues, against my emendation, that, on the contrary, *expert* is perfectly apposite; but that is because he has translated the phrase "im Richten erfahren," p. 132. However, he must inwardly realize that the Heb. *ṣedeq* simply cannot mean *Richten* ("judging"), for by the time he comes to p. 140 he goes back to the normal—but inept—"und sich auf Gerechtigkeit versteht." Moreover, the phrase I restored in this verse is, as I have since realized, the key to the original reading of the fifth and sixth words of Isa 1:17: rd. *šahǎru ṣedeq* "be zealous for equity" in view of the parallelism. (N.B. The syntax of MT in 16:5 is also wild: we should have expected *mahir b-*, cf. Prov 22:29; Ezra 7:6.)

YHWH. In it humble folk[45] may find refuge, (14:30a) and in his pasture[46] the poor may graze and the needy may lie secure. (16:6)[47] We have heard of Moab's pride—most haughty is he—of his pride and haughtiness and arrogance, of the iniquity in him."[48]

Of course nothing could be more characteristic of Isaiah than the thought that human pride is the root and essence of all sin: 2:11, 17; 3:16; 10:12–15. Characteristically, Zephaniah, preexilic and much influenced by Isaiah, predicts that YHWH will punish Judah's wicked neighbors for their pride, Zeph 2:8–10. He further predicts that Judah itself will be reduced to a blameless remnant by being purged of its "proudly exultant" ones. Those who remain will be "poor, humble folk," who will "take refuge" in the name of YHWH and will, like the poor and humble of Isa 14:30a in the above passage, "graze and lie down with none disturbing" (Zeph 3:11–13).

Micah the Morashtite, from Morashah by Gath (Mi 1:14), was a provincial who was so bitter over the corruption of the "rulers of the House of Jacob . . . chiefs of the House of Israel" (3:1–9) that he actually uttered the famous prediction (Mi 3:12): "Zion shall be plowed as a field, and Jerusalem become heaps of ruins, and the Temple Mount a wooded height woods." Since, however, according to Jer 26:18–19 YHWH was moved to revoke that decree by a great show of repentance on the part of King Hezekiah and his people, Micah may have retracted it. At any rate, Micah B (chs. 4–5),—which is at least in part preexilic ("and you will reach Babylon" in 4:10 is clearly a gloss), since 5:4–5 reflects the Assyrian period,—first contemplates a temporary removal of the kingship

---

[45] Rd. 'aniyye 'am' cf. Ps 72:4.

[46] Rd. bkaro; for kar cf. Isa 31:23 end; Ps 65:14.

[47] The gist of this verse is that Moab utterly lacks the requirements for admission that have just been cited from Isa 14:32, 30a.

[48] Bdyw is the suffixed form of bde (Nah 2:13; Hab 2:13; Job 39:25), which means "to, for, concerning, with"; so also Job 41:4. Other suffixed forms are bdy, Job 17:16; which both the Qumram Job Targum and the Septuagint rightly take to mean "with me," and bdyk, Job 11:3.

to Migdal-eder, 4:8, which may have been near Bethlehem (cf. Gen 35:19–21), while ch. 5 foresees the rise out of Ephrathah, the Bethlehem family which once produced David (I Sam 17:12; cf. Ruth 1:2; 4:11), a ruler who will be able to defend Judah against the Assyrians.

(b) Psalms 77, 80, 81

In light of the foregoing, it will of course never occur to us to assign any but a Judite origin to psalms like 2, 18, 20, 46, 48, 89, 132 or 144:1–11. But how about psalms which seem old yet feature "the older salvation history"? How about *Ps 77?* Is its concluding verse (77:21), "You guided Your people like a flock in the care of Moses and Aaron," prima facie evidence, in the absence of any signs of lateness, of an Israelian origin? It is; for a Judite would not have written (77:16), "With Your arm You redeemed Your people, the descendants of Jacob *and Joseph!"* This observation immediately suggests a scrutiny of *Ps 80,* which traces the history of the people (vv. 9–14) from the migration from Egypt, through the conquest and prosperous settlement, down to a present crisis. The sectional identity of the speakers is indicated at the outset by the cry, "Give ear, O Shepherd of Israel, who guided Joseph like a flock!" Here *Joseph* is not, as in 77:16, the name of an ancestor but a synonym of the ethnic designation *Israel* in the latter's more restricted sense of the league of central and northern tribes, just as in Amos 5:6, 15; 6:6 (in 6:1 too *bywsp* is no doubt to be read for *bsywn*) and already in II Sam 19:21. (Here the speaker is the Benjamite Shimei, who has brought with him 1,000 of his fellow tribesmen, II Sam 19:17–18.) Our psalm (Ps 80) would seem to date from even earlier, from premonarchic times in fact. "The man of Your right hand, the one whose arm You grasped" (v. 18, meaning "Your chosen one," cf. Isa 41:10, 13) may be either a premonarchic leader or the people personified. (The mutilated clause Ps 80:16b is obviously due to the wandering of a copyist's eye from the *ymynk* in v. 16 to that in v. 18, and is to be omitted.) As for the

date of the psalm's composition, it is the time of the struggle
against the Philistines that culminated in the disaster of Ebenezer, I
Sam 4. This appears, first of all, from the names of the tribes affected: "O You who are enthroned on the Cherubim, appear at the
head of *Ephraim, Benjamin, and Manasseh"* (Ps 80:2b–3aa).
Ephraim's involvement in that struggle follows from the location
of Shiloh in its territory, and Benjamin's from the fact that the
fugitive who brought the terrible news to Shiloh was a member of
that tribe (I Sam 4:12), while that of Manasseh is readily understandable from its proximity to Aphek and Ebenezer. An additional argument for this early dating may be the invocation of YHWH
as "You who sit on the Cherubim." For Eissfeldt[49] has made it
probable—from the fact that the sacred ark which was originally
housed in Shiloh and eventually found its way to Jerusalem is
described in full as "the Ark of (the Covenant of) YHWH ṢB'WT
who sits upon the Cherubim," I Sam 4:4; II Sam 6:4, and from the
fact that *YHWH ṢB'WT* (usually interpreted to mean 'YHWH of
Hosts') is actually attested as the name under which YHWH was
worshipped at Shiloh (I Sam 1:3, 11)—that the Deity was conceived
of in the Shiloh sanctuary as seated on a sphinx (cherub) throne
like those which are attested in ancient Near Eastern iconography,
and that the ark was somewhere nearby or under the throne. Now,
the Davidic monarchy had the ark, and it actually rested, in the
Jerusalem holy of holies, under a sort of seat formed by the touch-
ing tips of the inner wings of two giant cherubs that flanked it with
wings spread out sideways (I Ki 6:23–27; 8:4–6). That accounts for
the epithet "seated on the cherubs" surviving in Judah centuries
later (Ps 99:1; II Ki 19:15//Isa 37:16). But the nearest thing to a
cherub throne in post-Shiloh Joseph was, so far as the available
evidence goes, the golden calf instituted by Jeroboam I.

Likewise recalling the exodus-wilderness salvation history, and
likewise stemming from "Joseph," is Ps 81, which will be inter-

---

[49] O. Eissfeldt, *Kleine Schriften* III, 113–23; cf. p. 424 top.

preted later on, after we have examined the triumph of Josiah's reformation and its connection with Deuteronomy's festival calendar (Deut 16:1 ff.), and the latter's relations to earlier and later festival calendars.

(c) Psalm 47

One more *probable* Israelian psalm is Ps 47. Before we analyze it, let us recall that although neither Amos nor Hosea mentions any promise of the land of Canaan to the Patriarchs, Hosea does allude directly to some of the traditions about Jacob in Hos 12:3-5, 13 [12:2-4, 12],[49a] while Amos, who attests the use of "Isaac" as a designation of the Israelian nation (Amos 7:9, 16), indirectly attests some knowledge among the Israelians about the person Isaac by referring to a custom they had of making pilgrimages to Beersheba (Amos 5:5; 8:14). For Beersheba was the site of a shrine founded by Isaac when he experienced a theophany there (Gen 26:23-25; 46:1). One therefore wonders whether a similar early Israelian tradition about God having revealed himself to Abraham is reflected in the phrase "the people of the God of Abraham," Ps 47:10. I speak of an early Israelian tradition because of two links between this psalm and Amos: (1) *maśkil* in the sense of "song of adoration" occurs nowhere outside a psalm caption except in Ps 47:8 and, apparently, Amos 5:13 (which perhaps belongs between vv. 17 and 18); but above all, (2) the name "Pride of Jacob" for the Israelian homeland and nation is confined to Ps 47:5 and Amos 6:8, 8:7. Moreover, (3) Am 6:8, "I abhor the Pride of Jacob," looks uncannily like a deliberate contradiction of Ps 47:5, "the Pride of Jacob which he loves." We have observed before that Amos refutes the conclusions of his Israelian hosts from the salvation history that they keep repeating (Am 2:10, 9, 11 ff; 3:1-2;

[49a] Cf., on Hos 12, H.L. Ginsberg (above n. 22) and the already much cited JPS translation of *The Prophets*.

5:25; 9:7-8), but the repartee of Am 6:8 is considerably harsher.

That Ps 47 is early is confirmed by the fact that it is an enthrone-ment psalm, v. 9, and that it looks forward to Israelite victories and expansion, v. 5 (probably read *yarḥib:* "He will enlarge our land possession," cf. Exod 34:24; Deut 12:20). In view of the assertion that "YHWH is most high (*'elyon*), awesome," 47:3, and the climac-tic conclusion, "He is most exalted" (*m'od na'ăla*), v. 10, it seems that, in agreement with the plural imperatives "clap hands" and "acclaim" in v. 2, and the fivefold "sing a hymn" (*zammru*) in vv. 7-8,the *'ala* "has gone up" in v. 6 is to be emended to the plural imperative *'allu* "extol," even though the piel of *'ly* is otherwise attested only postbiblically. At the beginning of v. 10 *ndyby 'mym* is evidently equivalent, or to be emended, to *ndyby 'm* (cf. Num 21:18), the opposite of *'nyy 'm* "humble folk," (Ps 72:4), so that the verse means: "A princely folk are gathered, the people of the God of Abraham. For God's (people) are the nobles of the earth. He is most exalted." It would not even have been incongruous for such a hymn to be born just during Amos's ministry, in the days of the meteoric rise of Jeroboam son of Joash.

(d) Proverbs as an Israelian Book and the Role of King Hezekiah

M. Weinfeld[50] has called attention to some striking affinities between Deuteronomy and Proverbs, notably:

l' tsyg gbwl r'k 'šr gblw r'šwnym	*'l tsg gbwl 'wlm 'šr 'šw 'bwtyk*
You shall not move your neigh-bor's landmark, set up by pre-vious generations (Deut 19:14, cf. 27:17).	Do not move the ancient land-mark set up by your fathers (Prov 22:28; cf. 23:10).
You shall not have in your	Alternate weights and alternate

---

[50] *Deuteronomy and the Deuteronomic School* (above n. 24), pp. 260 ff.

pouch alternate weights (*'bn w'bn*), larger and smaller. You shall not have in your house alternate measures (*'yph w'yph*), a larger and a smaller. You must have honest, correct weights (*'bn šlmh*) and honest, correct measures. For everyone who deals dishonestly is abhorrent to YHWH (*tw'bt YHWH*) your God (Deut 25:12–16).

measures (*'bn w'bn 'yph w'yph*) are both alike abhorrent to YHWH (*tw'bt* YHWH), but correct weights (*'bn šlmh*) are his delight (Prov 11:1; cf. 20:10, 23).

But there are considerations in favor of going further and surmising that Proverbs itself is, like Deuteronomy, a book of Israelian origin. For one thing, there are some interesting echoes from it in Second Hosea. Kaufmann[51] has called attention to the fact that *dá'at 'ĕlohim,* which the prophet equates with *ḥésed* 'goodness' in Hos 4:1b; 6:6, recurs in Prov 2:5, as does also the variant *dá'at qdošim* in Prov 9:10; 30:3. *Qdošim,* by the way, is here a plural of majesty, or abstraction, like *'ĕlohim* 'deity', which is why Hosea employs it in parallel with *'el* in Hos 12:1 [11:12]. *Yd',* in all such phrases means 'to note, heed, or bear in mind,' a sense it can also have in other contexts, e.g. Isa 5:13, 19. The bare *dá'at* can mean the same thing as *dá'at 'ĕlohim.* That is why it is parallel to *yir'at* YHWH 'reverence for YHWH' in Prov. 1:29, as is also the full *dá'at 'ĕlohim* in Prov 2:5; and that is why in Hos 4:6 I emend, as the parallel or sequent of *haddá'at, torat 'ĕlohéka* to *yir'at 'ĕlohéka.* At the same time, this Hosean verse, which of course is an echo of Prov 1:29, illustrates the fact that the opposite of *yd'* in the sense of 'to be mindful of' is *škḥ* in the sense of 'to ignore' (rather than 'forget'); cf. Hos 2:15; 13:5. Still another Hosean borrowing from Proverbs 1 is the form *yšaḥărunni* 'they will look earnestly for me'

[51] Y. Kaufmann, *Toldot ha'emuna hayyiśr'elit* III, p. 124.

(regretting, in their distress, that they have ignored me), Hos 5:15, borrowed from Prov 1:25. Even the "but they will not find" of the Proverbs text originally also followed in Hosea; for Hos 5:6 originally followed 5:15; cf. 6:4–6. Cf. further Hos 7:9, "Strangers have consumed his, or its (i.e. the cake's), wealth," with Prov 5:10, "Lest strangers feast upon your wealth." And further, Hos 8:7, "For they sow wind, and they shall reap whirlwind," with Prov 22:7, "He who sows iniquity shall reap calamity."

But the very language of Proverbs may be evidence of an Israelian origin. It has been remarked that the first collection of Proverbs (chs. 1–9) is rich in words and forms that are known from Phoenician but not othwerwise, or only rarely, in Hebrew, and that such words are not altogether wanting in the rest of Proverbs; e.g. *ḥaruṣ* 'gold,' *qáret* (pausal form) 'city,' *ḥokmot* (singular, with original *-at* becoming *-ot* in accordance with the Phoenician rule for *a* followed by a single consonant in the last syllable of Phoenician nouns) 'wisdom,' *pw/yq* 'to find, obtain,' *ḥomiyyot* (so read in Prov 1:21) 'city walls.' Even the phrase *twʿbt YHWH* (lit. 'abhorrence of YHWH,' i.e.) 'abhorrent to YHWH,' which struck Weinfeld by its frequency in Proverbs and Deuteronomy (and absence from other books of the Bible; see above) has a striking parallel in the inscription on the sarcophagus of King Tibnit of Sidon[52] (ca. 500 B.C.E.): *k tʿbt ʿštrt hdbr h'* 'for such an act (i.e. opening or relocating the sarcophagus) is abhorrent to Astarte.'

Now, the penetration of Phoenician influences into the northern kingdom is more readily understandable than into the southern, in view of geography and of the presence of a Tyrian queen (Jezebel) at Jezreel and the penetration of the Tyrian Baal cult into certain circles in Ahab's kingdom (to a small extent also in Judah, through Ahab's sister Athaliah, II Ki 11:18a). But the decisive consideration is the part played in the "canonization" of Proverbs in Judah by

---

[52] Donner and Röllig, *Kanaanäische und Aramäische Inschriften*, No. 13.

King Hezekiah, Prov 25:1.[53] For the collecting of at least most of the material which we have identified as Israelian (and some more, such as the stories in the Books of Kings about Israelian kings and prophets) was probably in large part not a matter of pure chance but patronized by Hezekiah.

For the greater part of Hezekiah's reign (726–698) falls after the Assyrian capture of Samaria (722), and he evidently took the view that all the Israelian dynasties after Solomon had been illegitimate, the House of David being the only legitimate dynasty of Israel, and Judah being now the only surviving part of it. It is hardly an accident that just Micah, the prophet of the reign of Hezekiah (Jer 26:18), frequently says *Israel* where we should have expected *Judah*, Mi 1:13, 14; 3:1, 9 (cf. "Zion" and "Jerusalem" in vv. 10, 12). The religious reformation which Hezekiah carried out according to II Ki 18:4 was surely inspired by Deuteronomy, for in addition to abolishing the local shrines (*bamot*), he destroyed, among other cult objects, the cult post (*asherah*); and the only Pentateuch code which forbids keeping a cult post near the altar of YHWH is D: Deut 16:21. (Indeed, the only book of the Torah that mentions cult posts [asherim] at all is Deuteronomy, with the exception of Exod 34:17, which will be shown below to be dependent on Deuteronomy.)— As is well known, Hezekiah for a number of years up to 701 was in revolt against Assyrian suzerainty, and his allies included, in addition to Egypt, Tyre (as we know from Sennacherib's annals) and Babylon. He surely hoped to break the back of the Assyrian empire and to liberate the territories of what had been the "illegitimate"

---

[53] The exact sense of this verse is not immediately obvious. In view of the fact that the common notion behind all the derivatives of the root *'tq* seems to be that of advancing or raising, it may here imply either importing into Judah or depositing in a library. As for the relative clause, to take it as nondefining would be contrary to Hebrew idiom; if the writer had meant to imply that the preceding proverbs had *not* been "canonized" by the men of Hezekiah he would have been more likely to write here *wayya'tiqum 'anše ḥizqiyya* etc. I therefore prefer to render thus: "These too are Solomonic proverbs which were brought in by men of King Hezekiah of Judah."

kingdom of Israel. If he had succeeded, the inhabitants of that region would no doubt have readily agreed with him (1) that the Davidic dynasty, which had once been their own too, and which (unlike all the post-Solomonic dynasties of "Israel") was still in existence and had just liberated them, and which revered their prophets and observed their Torah, was also their legitimate dynasty, and (2) that the temple of Zion, which had been built by a king who was also theirs, was, unlike any of the northern sanctuaries, still standing and functioning and must therefore be "the site which your God YHWH will choose." But Hezekiah's grand scheme failed, and his successor Manasseh, no doubt regarding his father's religious policies as discredited, subjected Judah to a long reign of syncretism. The Torah which had been adopted by Hezekiah was forgotten until, seventy years later, there arrived a moment when it was opportune for it to be rediscovered, in a somewhat updated form.

IV. The Josian Reformation

(a) Evaluation of the Accounts in II Kings and II Chronicles

According to the account in II Ki 22:3—23:25, all of the reforms carried out by Josiah took place in the eighteenth year of his reign (622 B.C.E.), as a result of the discovery in the Temple of a book of teaching, which the priest Hilkiah handed to the scribe Shaphan, who read it (or from it?) to the king. Terribly shaken by the thought of how incensed YHWH must be with his people for its failure over a period of generations to obey the commandments of this book of teaching (*Torah*), Josiah sent a delegation of five top dignitaries to inquire of the prophetess Huldah. According to the account as we have it, she replied that all the terrible things that were threatened in the scroll (in the core of our ch 28, no doubt) would surely be fulfilled, but that because the monarch was so sincerely contrite it would not happen in his lifetime. We may surmise that the actual reply, unmodified *ex eventu,* was, "Since you are so sincerely repentant, purge the country in accordance with the requirements of the scroll, and the calamity will be averted." The Chronicler, II Chr 34, retains the story of the scroll find in Josiah's eighteenth year (vv. 8 ff.) and of the king's reaction to it, including the covenant he made with the people to abide by this scroll of teaching; but what is meant by the first clause in v. 33, "Josiah removed all the abominations in all the districts belonging to the Israelites," is not clear—since he has already related at length how this was done in the king's twelfth year, vv. 3b–7—unless the entire verse is merely a final summary of his reforms.

That Josiah actually carried out his main reforms (apart from the Deuteronomic Passover) in his twelfth regnal year (628 B.C.E.) was formerly widely believed because of the former belief that

39

Assyrian cults were imposed on vassals of Assyria, and it was
assumed that the death of Assyria's King Ashurbanipal (for which
one of the years that have been proposed is 627) would be seized as
a welcome opportunity for asserting independence by abolishing
those cults. This view of Assyrian policy has been effectively disposed of by Cogan,[54] yet even he assumes that an expedition by
Josiah did advance into northern Israel in his twelfth year.[55] In my
opinion, however, what we have here is one of those corrections of
tradition from subjective motives of which there are so many in
Chronicles. How, the Chronicler could not imagine, was it possible that Josiah tolerated "altars to all the host of heaven in both
courts of the House of YHWH" (II Ki 21:5) until he was twenty-six
years old? No, Manasseh, wicked as he was, was sufficiently chas-
tened, by an experience of being carried off in chains to Babylon,
to turn over a new leaf; and when YHWH heard his prayer and had
him returned to his kingship he anticipated every reform of Josiah
except the abolition of the local shrines (and even there, only
YHWH was worshipped). To be sure, Amon worshipped all the
carved images that his father Manasseh had worshipped, but we are
not told that he restored the altars of the astral cults (II Chr
33:10–23), so that when Josiah came to the throne the temple area,
at least, was free from abominations. But how about the country at
large? Surely, a pious man like Josiah could not tolerate it beyond
his twelfth regnal year, when he attained his majority (8 + 12 =
20). For twenty years is the age at which a male person becomes an
adult, cf. Num. 1:2, 20 ff. Although according to the normative
Halakah a Jew becomes subject to the full range of religious duties
on attaining puberty (12 years in a girl, 13 years in a boy), traces of
an older view, according to which it is the age of twenty years, are
not wanting.[56] And neither are reasons for doubting the historicity

---

[54] Morton Cogan, *Imperialism and Religion: Assyria, Judah and Israel in the Eighth and Seventh
Centuries B.C.E.* (Society of Biblical Literature Monograph Series, Vol. 19).
[55] Ibid., p. 71.
[56] L. Ginzberg, *An Unknown Jewish Sect*, New York 1976, pp. 45f.

of Josiah's depaganizing expedition of the year 628 or 627 B.C.E.

The account in II Ki. 22:2—23:25, in contrast, is psychologically persuasive. Josiah, who came to the throne as a boy of eight after 55 years of an unrepentant Manasseh whose policies were not changed during the two years of Amon, did not question the status quo during the first seventeen years of his reign. How it was possible to reconcile the worship of YHWH with the maintenance of astral cults in the courts of his own temple is suggested by Deut 17:2-7. This pericope is obviously a secondary expansion of the original D, since (1) it is directed against conditions that obtained in seventh-century Judah, not in eighth-century Israel-Ephraim,[57] and (2) the entire block Deut 16:21—17:7 interrupts the connection between Deut 16:18-20 and its continuation 17:8 ff. The pericope Deut 17:2-7, then, decrees death by lapidation for any man or woman who (v. 3) "has turned to the worship of other gods and bowed down to them, or to the sun or the moon or any of the heavenly host, something I never commanded." One naturally wonders why the astral bodies are not subsumed under "other gods" and why it should have been felt necessary to add the clause "something I never commanded." Ibn Ezra evidently asked himself these questions; for he explains that "other gods" means images, which are works of men, "the sun or the moon etc." are works of God, and "which I never commanded" means "which I never commanded [you] to worship, even though they are my own works." But we today are bound to ask a further question: do we know of any age that needed to have something so elementary impressed on it? We do, of course; it is the age of Josiah.

The difference between Hezekiah, who was orthoprax from the start, and Josiah, who only became converted (we have seen under what circumstances) after maintaining for seventeen years the

---

[57] On Am 5:26—which by the way surely belongs after 6:14—see Cogan (cf. above, n. 54), p. 104 top paragraph with pertinent notes. To judge by the silence of Deutero-Hosea, the Sakkut-Kaiwan cult was no longer of any importance in Israel after the fall of the Omri dynasty and the loss of Damascus.

paganizing status quo which he had inherited, is expressed by the *first* Deuteronomistic redactor of the Book of Kings, who wrote his history between the reformation of Josiah and the latter's death (622–609), with all the clarity one could wish for. His evaluation of Hezekiah reads (II Ki 18:5-6): "He trusted only in YHWH the God of Israel; there was none like him among all the kings of Judah after him, nor among those before him (since even the pious among them tolerated the local shrines). (6) . . . He kept the commandments which YHWH gave to Moses." His evaluation of Josiah, on the other hand, reads thus (II Ki 23:25): "There was no king like him before who *turned back* (note this expression!) to YHWH with all his heart and soul and might, in full accord with the Teaching of Moses; nor did any like him arise after him." (This last clause was probably added by the *second* Deuteronomistic redactor, after the fall of the monarchy.)

(b) The Pre-Deuteronomic Passover and Unleavened Bread Practices

(1) According to Exod 12:21-27; 13:2 ff.

Both the Kings and the Chronicles accounts report that Josiah made a covenant with the people to abide by the newly found book of teaching, and that he ordered them to observe the passover ritual as prescribed therein, i.e. at the one legitimate sanctuary, understood as that of Jerusalem. Because the Kings account says nothing about the week of unleavened bread, while Deut 16 lacks any requirement that it be observed at the sanctuary, de Vaux,[58] to whom its observance away from the sanctuary was for some reason unthinkable, believed that Josiah's Deuteronomy prescribed only the observance of Passover and that the present Deut 16:1 ff. was confused. However, the text of Deut 16 is not confused, if one

---

[58] R. de Vaux, *Les sacrifices de l'Ancien Testament*, Paris 1964, 7, 24 f.; English translation (made from manuscript): *Studies in Old Testament Sacrifice*, Cardiff 1964, 1, 23 f.

compares it with the older practice and asks oneself what made D modify it. The older practice is reflected in the pre-Deuteronomic passages of Exod 12–13 plus 23:14–19. I will classify this material as E, but understanding E as meaning not "Elohist(ic)"—a term which has become problematic—but Ephraim(ite). For the close connection between the E of Exodus and Numbers on the one hand and Deuteronomy on the other—even apart from their common polemic against the specifically Israelian cult object the golden calf, Exod 32–34//Deut 9:8—10:11—points to an Israelian origin of the former. In Exod 12:21–27, then, the Israelites are instructed to slaughter passover offerings of sheep and goats (ṣon), apply some of their blood to the lintel and to the two doorposts of each man's house, and stay indoors until morning. This would seem to imply that the slaughtering takes place before nightfall, as does perhaps also the cooking, if (as it seems reasonable to suppose) the meat was to be consumed: cf. the P instruction above in v. 8. The people are informed that when YHWH passes through Egypt that night to smite the Egyptians, he will protect against entry by the destroyer any entrance which is marked with the blood. (For pasaḥ 'to protect' cf. Isa 31:55.) From here on everything is clear: this same ritual is to be observed to the end of time, so that every father can impress on his children that it was in this way that YHWH passed over, or—better—protected, the *houses* of the Israelites "when he smote the Egyptians but saved our *houses*." As for the date on which the ritual is to be observed, that is only specified many hours later: in Exod 13:4, to which we shall come presently. [See Addenda.]

The E account is continued in 12:29, 30, the second sentence from *watthi* on (the cry is to be understood to have gone up when the Egyptians arose in the morning), and then vv. 33–39 (cf. 11:1–8): On arriving at Succoth, on the border of Egypt, the Israelites baked unleavened cakes of the dough which they had snatched up, along with the bowls in which it had been kneaded, and had wrapped on their shoulders with their cloaks, and which had failed to rise in the meantime. Next comes 13:2 ff.: (3) And

Moses said to the people, "Remember this day, on which you went free from Egypt, the house of bondage—how YHWH freed you from it with a mighty hand—as a day on which no leavened bread is to be eaten. (4) You go free on this day, on the new moon[59] of milky grain.[60] (5) So, when YHWH has brought you into the land

---

[59] A. B. Ehrlich, *Randglossen zur hebräischen Bibel,* Leipzig, I (1928), 312–313. Ehrlich argued that wherever the combination *ḥdš h'byb* occurs the context requires an exact calendar date, which is obtained when one takes *ḥódeš* in its well attested sense of *new moon.* Against de Vaux's objections, it may be added, firstly, that this sense of *ḥódeš* is not limited to early sources (I Sam 20:5, 18; II Ki 4:23; Isa 1:13; Amos 8:5 [in connectin with which see also *Eretz Israel* 3 (1954), 83f.]) but is still very much alive in Num 28:14; 29:6; Isa 66:23, Ezek 46:1, 3, 6 and, secondly, that early biblical Hebrew has no other means of expressing the concept "new moon." (For this, priestly sources commonly use [*b*]*'ehad laḥódeš,* Lev 23:24; Num 29:1; Ezek 45:18, and postbiblical Hebrew says *roš ḥódeš,* the plural of which [*raše ḥódašim*] occurs already in Num 10:10.)

[60] This meaning of *'abib* was pointed out by G. Dalman, *Arbeit und Sitte in Palästina* I/2, pp. 416 (lower half), 455 ff.; III, pp. 8, 10. His proofs are: (1) Saadiah, not only in the combination *ḥódeš ha'abib* but also in Exod 9:12 and Lev 2:14, renders *'abib* by the Arabic word *farik* '(what is easily) hulled by rubbing (i.e. between the fingers)'; and (2) from Mishnah Kil'ayim 5:7, it is clear that *'abib* is a stage in the growth of cereals between mere stalks (*'asabim*) with no spikes, or ears, on them and fully ripe cereal (*dagan*). In III, p. 1, Dalman notes that the change from soft-seeded ears to fully ripe ones is marked by a change in the color of the standing grain: barley turns from green to yellow; in wheat, the green fades to a shade that is as light as to be almost white. I have learned further from competent informants in Jerusalem that during the green phase of the standing grain the seeds in the ears are likewise green and that if they are pressed liquid will ooze from them, for which reason this stage is called *havšalat ḥalav,* literally 'milk ripening,' in Ivrit. It is this term that has inspired my own coinage *milky grain.*
Of course milky grain, though it cannot be ground to flour, is not unusable as food. Christian Arabs in Jerusaelm have informed me that wheat in this stage is cooked and eaten under the colloquial name of *frike;* cf. Hans Wehr, *Dictionary of Modern Literary Arabic* s.v. *farik.* *Further,* a combination of Lev 2:14, which speaks of a cereal offering of first fruits, with Mishnah Menaḥot 10:4, which speaks of the *'ómer* of Lev 23:9ff. (to be discussed in ch. VII), suggests that milky grain of barley could also be rendered palatable by parching and grinding to grits.
It is too bad that Dalman's observation (Vol. I/2 was first printed in 1928, Vol. III in 1933) has apparently hitherto gone unnoticed. As a matter of fact, Dalman himself somehow failed to realize that his observation precludes his theory about the original character of the season of unleavened bread (I/2, 489–453), which is based on the generally accepted view that it was a grain harvest festival (probably, de Vaux [see above n. 58] and some others add, borrowed from the Canaanites), in which the unleavened bread was baked with flour from the new crop—from which no flour can be produced while it is in the *'abib* stage as Dalman himself defines it! An additional argument against the generally accepted view will be encountered presently.

... which he swore (to your fathers)[61] to give you ... you shall observe on this new moon the following practice. (6) Six days you shall eat unleavened bread, and on the seventh day there shall be a pilgrimage for YHWH. (7) Throughout the seven days unleavened bread shall be eaten; no leavened bread of yours and no leaven of yours shall be seen in all your territory. (8) ... (9) ... (10) you shall keep this institution at its set time from year to year."

Note well that it is only for the *seventh* day (v. 6) that a pilgrimage is prescribed; for the *first* day, as we have seen, *the passover*—a *household* sacrifice—is prescribed.

(2) According to Exod 23:14-19

In Exod 15:20—19:2, the progress of the Israelites is traced from Succoth to the scene of revelation. In the E source, which is followed by D, the general locality in which the revelation took place is called Horeb, and the actual mountain of revelation is called the Mountain of God, Exod 3:1; 4:27; 17:6; 18:5, while in P the general locality is called the Wilderness of Sinai and the mountain Mount Sinai, Exod 19:1, 11, 18, 23. Of the various pieces of legislation that are reported to have been promulgated here, the most important one for us is the one that is designated in Exod 24:3a, 4 as "the words of YHWH," in 24:3b as "the words that YHWH uttered," and in 24:8 as "these words." The words in question were, according to 24:4-8, reduced to writing by Moses, who made them the basis of a covenant between YHWH and Israel which he himself solemnized by means of an appropriate ceremony.

To begin with the ceremony, it seems obvious to me that it has not been transmitted quite accurately. To have dashed part of the blood on the people (v. 8a) would have been (1) messy in addition to requiring an enormous quantity of blood; (2) inconsistent, since the people themselves do not correspond logically to the

---

[61] The phrases "to your fathers" here and "and to your fathers" in v. 11 are doubtless glosses.

altar—representing YHWH—on which the other part of the blood
was dashed; and (3) it would have left otiose the 12 pillars representing the 12 tribes of Israel. My conclusion is that what was originally related was that the pillars represented Israel precisely for the
purpose of receiving the dashed blood just as the altar had represented YHWH for that purpose. [The first two of my above three
difficulties with the account in its received form were sensed by Ibn
Ezra, whose solutions, however, (based on Lev 3: 13–15 and 8:30)
are forced. I surmise that if it had occurred to him he would have
considered it legitimate to solve all three of the difficulties by the
single stroke of commenting on the phrase "upon the people" in
Exod 24:8 as follows: "It means the twelve pillars; for they sym-
bolize (in Ibn Ezra Hebrew, perhaps *ky hn zkrwn/mzkrt l*) the twelve
tribes of Israel."]

What is more important is that the phrase "and all the rules"
(*w't kl hmšptym*) which follows "all the words of YHWH" at the end
of v. 3 is an interpolation, since it is wanting after the other mentions of the said "words" in 3b, 4, and 8 end. Its purpose is to
include the "rules" (*mišpaṭim*) of 21:1–23:9 in the covenant of
24:3–8; but that was not the original intention of this passage. For
the E elements in 24:12–18; 31:18—34:28, which relate how
Moses went up to the Mountain of God for forty days and nights in
order to receive "the tablets of stone on which I have inscribed the
teachings and commandments to instruct them," conclude by
revealing that the tablets contained nothing other than "the terms
of the covenant, the Ten Words" (34:28), and this phrase can only
refer to "The First Ritual Decalogue,"[62] Exod 23:10–27.

---

[62] This term, as also (so far as I know) the very discovery that Exod 23:10 ff. is a decalogue,
is my own. The practice has hitherto been—in emulation of Johannes Wolfgang Goethe,
*Zwo wichtige bisher unerörtete biblische Fragen, zum ersten Mal gründlich beantwortet von einem Land-
geistlichen in Schwaben,* dated Feb. 6, 1773—to speak of "*The* Ritual Decalogue" and to apply
this term to the covenant of Exod 34:10–27. But *the whole of Exod 34:10–27 is an interpolation*
which owes its existence to a *post-Deuteronomic* writer, as will be demonstrated in Chapter VI.
Note, therefore, that Exod 34:1 says that YHWH—not, like v.27, that Moses—will write on
the tablets, and that without the intrusion of vv. 10–27 the natural referent of "and he
wrote" in v.28b is the "YHWH" of v.28a. It follows that "the terms of the Covenant, the Ten
Words" means the ritual decalogue of 23:10ff., whose constituent elements are identified p.

This document comprises ten ritual precepts for Israel (I, 23:10–11; II, v.12; III, v.13; IV, v.15; V, v.16a; VI, v.16b; VII, v.18a; VIII, v.18b; IX, v.19a; X, v.19b) followed by vv. 20–33, an undertaking by YHWH to bring Israel safely to Canaan, expel its present inhabitants, and enable Israel to live in it happily—provided it does not take over any cult sites or practices from those aborigines.

Those of this Decalogue's precepts which deal with pilgrimages are nos. IV–X, comprising vv. 15–19; and they are preceded by a special heading of their own, v. 14. We shall break this block up into Sections followed by comments.

(14) You shall make pilgrimages to me on three occasions in the year.

Precept IV (v.15). The First Pilgrimage

The Pilgrimage of Unleavened Bread you shall observe, as I have (already) commanded you, after eating unleavened bread for seven days at the set time of the new moon of milky grain—because it was on the latter that you came out of Egypt—and none shall appear before me empty-handed.

Comment

"As I have (already) commanded you" can only refer to 13:4–9, which we have already dealt with and in connection with which we have noted that when 13:6 prescribes a pilgrimage for the *seventh* of

---

47, top. [At the end of the Deuteronomic adaptation (Deut 9:8–10:5) of the E account (Exod 32–34 minus interpolations) of the golden calf episode, namely in Deut 10:4, the expression "the Ten Words" is taken over from Exod 34:28; but in Deut 10:4 it is naturally redefined as referring to "the Ethical Decalogue" (the classical "Ten Commandments," Deut 5:6–17), which constituted the Covenant of Horeb according to Deut 5:3–5, 18a. From Deut 10:4, in turn, the expression "the Ten Words" was copied in 4:51 (which is part of *the later introduction* to D, Deut 1:1—4:43), where it is of course likewise to be understood as "the Ethical Decalogue."]

the seven days beginning with the new moon of milky grain it means precisely the seventh. Since a pilgrimage means a visit to a sanctuary, the legislator here adds "and none shall appear before me empty-handed."

Since the passover ritual does not involve, in pre-Deuteronomic times, a pilgrimage, it is not mentioned here, among the pilgrimages. However, we shall see that it does figure in the appendix, vv. 17–19.

Precept V (v.16a). The Second Pilgrimage

Also the Pilgrimage of the Harvest, of the first fruits of (the portion of) your produce which you sow in the field.

Comment

This means the first grain that you reap. The pilgrimage must be made, according to this text, at the very beginning of the grain harvest, not, as is gratuitously assumed in light of the other festival calendars, seven weeks later. Since barley ripens from 10 to 14 days earlier than wheat does in the same locality, the first fruits offered on this pilgrimage necessarily consisted of barley. [Why its original date was postponed seven weeks and its original name correspondingly changed to Pilgrimage of Weeks (Deut 16:9–10), will be discussed in due course.] If our calendar dates the *second* pilgrimage at the beginning of the harvest, it cannot be doing the same for the first pilgrimage—an additional reason for, once for all, dissociating the season of unleavened bread from the harvest and rejecting any suggestion that the unleavened bread had to be baked with flour from the new crop—at a stage when it could not yet yield

---

[62a] Even writers who had not benefited by the discoveries of Ehrlich on *ḥódeš* and Dalman on *'abib* (and who of course could not have benefited by my observation that in Exod 23:14 ff. it is the *second* pilgrimage that is dated at the beginning of the grain harvest, and that,

flour![62a] Presumably, since no calendar date is given, and grain ripens at different dates in different sections of the country (and not at the same date every year), every farmer chose his own date for presenting his first fruits.

Precept VI (v.16b). The Third Pilgrimage

Lastly, the Pilgrimage of Ingathering, at the beginning[63] of the year, when you gather in your produce from the field.

In determining just what date our half-verse Exod 23:16b has in mind, we are helped to a wholly unexpected extent[63a] by the Gezer Calendar Inscription.[64] In this epigraph, a total of eight principal agricultural labors are apportioned among the months of the year. Four of these labors are preceded by the word *yrḥw* and four by *yrḥ,* and a total of twelve months is obtained if *yrḥw* is taken as some sort of dual (or possibly plural) form.[64a] The ingathering will

---

since the Pilgrimage of Unleavened Bread is listed before it, it must on that account too be dated *before* the grain harvest), might have been given pause by the following considerations: (1) there is no record of any requirement by any sect that the *maṣṣot* of the *maṣṣot* season be baked with flour from the new crop; (2) on the contrary, every known sect has restrictions on the use of flour from the new crop during the week of *maṣṣot*; and (3) even Pharisaic Judaism, which is the most liberal in permitting flour from the new crop, forbids it for the first day of the season of unleavened bread. Yet the only recent writer who, to my knowledge, has resisted the notion that the flour for the festival of unleavened bread must be derived from the new crop is J. B. Segal, *The Hebrew Passover,* London 1963. He is to be lauded.

[63] Since instead of our *bṣet haššana* Exod 34:22 has *tqupat haššana,* we are reminded of Ps 19:7, in which the beginning of the sun's course across the sky is spoken of as its *moṣa* while its conclusion is spoken of as its *tqupa*; and we further recall II Chron 24:23, where *tqupa* is the completion of a year, and Isa 29:1 and Job 1:5, where the cognate verb *nqp* means 'to go by' said of a period of time.

[63a] But see Albright toward the end of the article cited below in n. 64a.

[64] Donner-Röllig (see above, n. 52), no. 182.

[64a] For the justification of this interpretation two hypotheses are available:
    (1) that of W.F. Albright, BASOR 92 (1943), 16–26;
    (2) that of J.B. Segal, JSS 7 (1962), 212–21.
On the Albright hypothesis, *yrḥw* is to be read *yarḥēw* and to be translated "His two months are," while *yrḥ* is to be read *yarḥo* and to be translated "His month is." Segal, on the other hand, claims that where previous scholars have read *yrḥw* the fourth sign is not a *w* at all but an approximation to the Egyptian sign for the numeral 2. Both papers deserve a careful

include that of olives, the picking of which is not specially mentioned. The calendar's two months of ingathering correspond
roughly to October and November.

Whenever the actual labor of ingathering began, the official
month always began on a new moon. (Whether or not anything
like the Babylonian practice of intercalation was practiced, we do
not know.) The official beginning of the ingathering season therefore fell on a new moon, and since that season was the first in the
year, its official beginning would have been the beginning of a *new
year*. But it would seem that the actual *pilgrimage* of the season of
ingathering was observed two weeks later, on the day of the *full
moon*.[65] For our remaining Joseph psalm, Ps 81, reads (if we disregard the late caption v.1) as follows:

"(2) Acclaim the God who is our strength, raise a shout for the
God of Jacob. (3) Utter song and sound the timbrel, the melodi-
ous lyre and the harp. (4) Blow the horn on the new moon, on the
full moon for the day of our pilgrimage. (5) For it is a law for
Israel, a rule of the God of Jacob, (6) which he established as an
institution in Joseph when he came forth over the land of Egypt.

"I heard a language I knew not." (7–8, YHWH addresses Israel,
reviewing his acts of grace toward it in Egypt and in the wilderness,
and continues,) "(9) Hear, my people, and I will admonish you: O
Israel, do[66] listen to me. (10) There shall be no foreign god in your
midst, you shall not bow down to an alien god. (11) I YHWH am
your God who brought you up from the land of Egypt. Open wide
your mouth, and I will fill it."[67] (Vv. 12 ff., which may be an addi-

---

perusal by the serious student; but since my following reconstruction of the history of the
Hebrew autumn pilgrimage is compatible with either of them, I defer a decision between
them.

[65] In the same way as, in the final ("priestly") calendar, the "holy occasion commemorated by loud blasts" (Lev 23:24) is the first day of the seventh month, but the pilgrimage of
booths (*sukkot*) takes place on the *fifteenth* (or full moon) day of that month (Lev 23:23–25,
33–36, 39–42; Num 29:1–6; 12–38).

[66] For this force of *'im* followed by the second person of the imperfect, cf. perhaps Prov
24:11.

[67] A very timely promise in the season of ingathering.

tion, go on to say that Israel did not listen, and so YHWH forsook them. But if only they would listen, he would humble their enemies.) V.17 repeats the promise that is so timely just in the season of ingathering: "I would feed him with the richest wheat, I would sate him with honey from the rock."

Exod 23:17-19 is an appendix to the festival calendar vv. 14-16, and, since v.17, which takes up again the introduction v.14, uses instead of the rare *rgalim* 'times'[68] the common *p'amim,* it may well be by a later hand. At the same time, the appendix in no wise contradicts vv. 14-16, and may therefore be assigned to the same "school" as those verses and dubbed E². What it adds to vv. 4-16 is rules for the observance of each of the three pilgrimages. But v.18 is a *double* addition to v.15; accordingly, proceed thus:

Precept VII (v.18a):

You shall not shed the blood of my offering while leavened bread still exists.

Precept VIII (v.18b):

And the suet of my pilgrimage sacrifice shall not be left lying until morning.

Comment

Largely because in the parallel verse Exod 34:25 the second clause specifically names the passover offering, it is usually supposed that both clauses refer to the passover offering in our verse as well. However, in this as in many other features, Exod 34:11-26 is influenced by Deuteronomy, which, as we shall see presently,

---

[68] This word occurs apart from Exod 23:14 only in Num 22:28, 32, 33, there too with the numeral 3. It evidently could only be used with 3, just as *monim,* Gen 31:7, 41, could only be used with 10.

abolishes the pilgrimage of the seventh day and instead converts the passover offering of the first night from a home ritual into a pilgrimage sacrifice. Our Exod 23:18, on the other hand, still retains the passover offering of Exod 12:21–27 as a home ritual and designates it by the same word—*zébaḥ*—as 12:26. It too doubtless contemplates for it a slaughtering some time before the advent of the night of the new moon of milky grain; and for the pilgrimage sacrifice of the seventh day, it retains the word *ḥag* of 13:6. In the view of our passage, when the Israelite slaughters—at home—his pascal *zébaḥ*, he can only be sure that no leavened bread of his own is still extant; when, however, he offers his pilgrimage sacrifice at the sanctuary on the seventh day, he must make sure that the suet—which as in all communion sacrifices was placed on the altar to burn away (no doubt more or less as prescribed in Lev 3)—has been disposed of before the morning of the eighth day. For some people will surely put up some dough to rise not many hours after the season of unleavened bread has expired at the sunset of the seventh day, and by morning leavened bread will have reappeared in the land. Of course, the high flammability of suet makes this precept easy to comply with.

Precept IX (v.19a):

That Precept IX merely explicates Precept V is obvious.

Precept X (v.19b):

As for the bearing of Precept X—the prohibition against boiling a (male) kid in the milk of its dam—[69] on Precept VI, if I am not

---

[69] The boiling of lamb and kid meat in milk is attested by both L. Bauer and N. Glueck; see U. Cassuto, *Enṣiqlopedia Miqra'it* II, 436–7. As for the principle behind the biblical prohibition, which seems to be aimed only at the milk of the young animal's own dam, it is patently the same one as is embodied in the prohibitions against taking possession of a wild mother bird along with her eggs or fledglings (Deut 22:6–7) and against slaughtering a domestic ruminant (probably a female one is meant) and its young on the same day (Lev 22:28).

mistaken, it is this: It does not pay to raise to maturity more male kids than will be needed for breeding purposes, since the mature he-goat, unlike the ram, yields neither wool nor palatable meat. Accordingly, it was doubtless a common practice to dispose of one's surplus male kids during the festive season of ingathering.[70] (The fully grown female, of course, is prized for her milk.)

The foregoing, then, is the status quo that the Deuteronomist knew. Before going on, however, to see how he modified it, and why, we may here answer an obvious question. Having proved that the season of unleavened bread always began with the passover offering, and that it has nothing to do with the grain harvest, can I suggest any alternative theory of its origin? I can: it was merely a token prolongation of the passover meal; see, immediately below, Deut 16:3. And as for the origin of the passover ritual, the observations of Dhorme[71] have convinced a majority of writers that the full description in Exod 12:5-11 points unmistakably to a nomad or semi-nomad origin. The features noted are: the victims—sheep and goats to the exclusion of bovines, which are not bred by Bedouin; the requirement of roasting, which is the manner of preparation of the Bedouin, who cannot be encumbered with a lot of pots; the unleavened bread, which is the staple food of Bedouin; the accompanying *mrorim,* which are wild aromatic herbs with which Bedouin are wont to season their food; and above all, the manner of slaughtering—without benefit of altar, sanctuary, or priest—which has passed on into official Islam. Further, the smearing of the entrance with the blood of the victim has been compared to the apotropaic smearing of tents and houses with blood by the sedentarized Bedouin of Moab, and parallels have even been found both among Arabs and others to the preservation of the wholeness

[70] G. Dalman, *Arbeit u. Sitte* VI, remarks (p. 186) that though far more goats are kept (for their milk) than sheep, less than half as many are slaughtered, because the meat of these scrawny animals is not very tempting, and (p. 189) that male kids are frequently slaughtered, because only a small number of he-goats is needed.

[71] E. Dhorme, *L'Evolution religieuse d'Israel,* I. *La Religion des Hébreux nomades* (1937), pp. 211-12.

of the bones (Exod 12:46; Num 9:12). A recent writer, Henninger,[72] repeats the view he has previously defended (and which was already put forward by Ewald in 1840) that the passover offering is related to the Rajab feasts of pre-Islamic Arabia. In Rajab, which was originally a spring month, even pastoral Arabs used to repair to sanctuaries which had sprung up in the vicinities of the market towns at which they bought their grain. There, it is true, they would immolate (for the priests of Arab sanctuaries were not slaughterers but custodians and diviners) and consume (it is believed) the firstborn of their flocks, which the biblical pascal victims (*pace* Wellhausen and Henninger) were not; but I find fascinating the fact that the festival began on a new moon and lasted eight days.[73] Is the resemblance to the passover offering of the new moon of milky grain and its token continuation for seven days fortuitous, or is it significant?

---

[72] Joseph Henninger, S.V.D., *Les Fêtes de Printemps chez les Sémites et la Pâque Israélite (Etudes Bibliques)*, Gabalda, Paris 1975.

[73] J. Wellhausen, *Reste arabischen Heidentums*²(³), 1897 (1927), 94–101, especially p. 98 middle with footnote 1.

V. The Deuteronomic Reformation
of the Festival Calendar:
Deut 16:1–17

1. Passover-Unleavened Bread, vv.1–8, 12

(1) Observe the new moon of milky grain and offer a passover sacrifice to your God YHWH; for it was on the new moon of milky grain, at night, that your God YHWH freed you from Egypt. (2) Slaughter a passover sacrifice for your God YHWH, from the flock and the herd, in the place where YHWH will choose to establish his name. (3) You shall not eat anything leavened with it; for seven days you shall eat on account of it unleavened bread, bread of stress—for you departed from the land of Egypt hurriedly—so that you may remember the day of your departure from the land of Egypt as long as you live. (4) For seven days no leaven of yours shall be seen in all your territory. None of the flesh of what you slaughtered on the evening of the first day shall be left until morning. (5) You are not permitted to slaughter the passover sacrifice in any of the settlements that your God YHWH is giving you, (6) but only at the place where your God YHWH will choose to establish his name shall you slaughter the passover sacrifice—in the evening, at sundown, the time of day when you departed from Egypt. (7) Having boiled and eaten it at the place which your God YHWH will choose, in the morning you may start back on your journey home. (8) But you shall eat unleavened bread for six (more) days, and on the seventh day (observe) a concluding solemnity[74] for your God YHWH, when you shall do no work. (12) Bear

---

[74] This is what *'ăṣéret* means as an *absolute* form (Lev 23:36; Num 29:35); of course it can also be the construct state of *'ăṣara* 'assemblage'; see Jer 9:1.

in mind that you were a slave in Egypt, and be careful to obey these
laws.

Comments

   Why I moved up v. 12 from its present position at the conclusion
of the paragraph on the Pilgrimage of Weeks, is obvious; it motivates the observance of the rituals that commemorate the deliver-
ance from Egypt, not the Pilgrimage of Weeks.[74a] The changes
introduced by D into the passover-unleavened bread observances
were dictated by its fundamental innovation of the centralization of
the cult. The old manner of observing the passover ritual could not
be retained, since it was a cultic slaughtering, requiring ritual
purity, whereas D was as strict about forbidding cultic slaughtering
"in your settlements" as he was liberal in permitting profane
slaughtering. Twice we are admonished that any domestic
ruminants slaughtered "in your settlements" shall be partaken of
"by clean and unclean alike, just like the gazelle and the deer"
(Deut 12:25, cf. 22). On the other hand, it was probably felt that it
was too well established—probably observed by more Israelites
than the pilgrimage of the seventh day was even in the days of a
multiplicity of legitimate sanctuaries—to be abolished. (We may
well wonder how many people observed all of the pilgrimages year
after year even in pre-Deuteronomic times.) D's solution was
therefore to move the passover sacrifice from the home to the one
legitimate sanctuary. Here, of course, the rituals of smearing the
entrance of one's house with the blood and staying inside one's
house for at least a token part of the night had to be dispensed
with. So, having brought the Israelite to the sanctuary, D had him

---

[74a] Stephen A. Kaufman, *Maarav,* I/2 (Spring 1979), p. 132 top, plausibly argues that it
motivates the inclusion of one's slaves in the celebration (v. 11); but v. 16, by limiting the
duty of "confronting" YHWH at the chosen site three times a year to "all your males,"
shows that it realizes that even the requirement to take along one's own family is only a
pious wish.

wait until sunset so that the slaughtering would be done within the season of unleavened bread, and then it could simply take the place of the pilgrimage sacrifice of the seventh day of that season. For it will be noticed that the pilgrimage of the seventh day is abolished, though the day itself retains a special character as a concluding solemnity. Thus the passover sacrifice becomes a communion sacrifice in everything but the name and the unusual hour. That indeed is why our passage does not specify a male lamb or kid but permits sheep, goats, or cattle with no restrictions of age and sex; and that is why it prescribes boiling, which is the usual way of preparing communion sacrifices. In order to justify the unusual hour of slaughtering, tradition is modified so as to make sunset the hour at which the exodus began (vv. 1, 6). (For even according to P, who has the Egyptians discover their casualties in the middle of the night [Exod 12:30a] and has Pharaoh summon Moses and Aaron forthwith and grant them permission to leave [Exod 12:31–32], the Israelites did not actually depart until broad daylight, Num. 33:3.) I have been using everywhere the somewhat awkward "new moon of milky grain" in order to avoid making a proper name of the word 'abib; for we simply do not know what the month which began with that new moon was called—or indeed whether it was always the same month, since the text seems to mean the first new moon that is due after the first ears of grain appear, which does not happen at exactly the same time every year.

Of course, when all the sources were eventually combined in the single Torah that we know, an attempt to reconcile our passage with Exod 12:5 ff. was bound to be made. *Ḥódeš ha'abib* was a very minor difficulty, since *ḥódeš* could be taken in the sense of 'month' and it could be assumed that the same month was meant as in Exod. 12:2,6,18 and in the priestly literature generally; but the terms 'from the flock and from the herd' and the boiling were harder to dispose of. As is well known, the rabbinic solution is that only the animals from the flock are for passover offerings, while those from the herd are for the pilgrimage offerings which are obligatory at every pilgrimage, and that *ubiššalta,* Deut 16:7, means

not 'you shall boil' but 'you shall cook in fire' (i.e. 'you shall
roast'); see Mekilta to Exod 12:5 and 9 and Sifre on Deut 16:2. But
the same harmonization is presupposed in the account of Josiah's
passover in II Chron 35, as was realized by Pseudo-Rashi on the
chapter. Of modern writers, Rudolph[75] interprets the Chronicler's
account correctly in the main, since he realizes that the *qodašim* of II
Chr 35:13 must refer to the *baqar* (domestic bovines) of vv. 7, 8, 9,
only the male lambs (*kbašim*) and male kids (*bne 'izzim*), v.7, being
psaḥim. All that might have been added was a specific statement that
the account is the result of a conscious harmonization of Deut 16
with Exod 12, plus the above references to Mekilta and Sifre, and
an observation that Targum Onqelos, which regularly renders the
Hebrew *zébaḥ šlamim* by *niksat qudšin/qudšayyà* (e.g. Lev 3:1,3,6,9),
translates Deut 16:2 exegetically as follows: *wtikkos pišà . . . min bne
'ànà wniksat qudšayyà min tore* 'and you shall slaughter the passover
sacrifice . . . from the young males of the flock and the *qudšayyà*
sacrifice from the herd.' Clearly, *happésaḥ . . . whaqqodašim*, II Chr
35:13 = *pišà . . . wniksat qudšayyà,* Onqelos to Deut 16:2, and
whaqqodašim there means 'and the communion sacrifices.'

2. The Pilgrimage of Weeks, Deut 16:9–11

(9) You shall count off seven weeks; start counting off seven
weeks when the sickle is first put to the standing grain.

(10) Then you shall observe a Pilgrimage of Weeks for your God
YHWH, offering your freewill contribution according as your God
YHWH has blessed you. (11) And you shall rejoice before YHWH
with your son and daughter, your male and female slave, the Levite
in your settlements and the stranger, the fatherless, and the widow
in your midst, at the place where your God will choose to establish
his name.

Comment. I have already pointed out that a seven-week interval

---

[75] W. Rudolph, *Chronikbücher (Handbuch zum AT, Erste Reihe 21)* 1955.

after the beginning of the reaping of the grain crop is *not* contemplated by Exod 23:16a. But the centralization of the cult created a problem of logistics. With the reaping, the busiest season in the year begins for the farmer. Between the demands of his work and the midday heat, it must have been hard enough for him to travel to and from one of the not too distant sanctuaries in the days when more than one were permitted; the centralization of the cult made it simply unfeasible for all but those who lived reasonably near the one legitimate temple. That is why D introduces the seven-week delay—it's much easier once all the grain is on the threshing floor. The writer of vv. 9–11 does not pretend that his Pilgrimage of Weeks is something that has long been current, in the manner in which E speaks of *the* Pilgrimage of the Grain Harvest, Exod 23:16a, but frankly says "you shall observe *a* Pilgrimage of Weeks (*hag šabu'ot,* rather than *'et hag haššabu'ot*), and he doesn't even make it a pilgrimage of first fruits (no particular festival is named in connection with the first fruits ceremony of Deut 26:1–11, and the rabbinic view that it means sometime between the second and third pilgrimage festivals may be the actual intention), and perhaps a money gift will do.—Rejoicing, which is not prescribed for the passover-maṣṣot pilgrimage, is enjoined for this one at its new date and for the following one, no doubt because they were traditional seasons of merrymaking.[76]—Since the day on which the first grain becomes ripe for the sickle varies from year to year and from place to place, perhaps the intention is that the day of the start of the count-off shall be determined for every village by its sheik or by a town meeting. But it is not impossible that each man is guided by the day on which his own grain ripened.

[76] My interpretation of Ps 4:7–8 is: (7) The many (meaning "the masses" as, e.g., in Mal 2:6, 8, where *tora* means 'priestly rulings') said, "Who will grant us bounty? Extend (read *nṭh* [*nṭe*], cf. Gen 39:21) to us the light of Your countenance, O YHWH." (8) And You brought joy to their hearts, when (rd. *blibbam 'et*) their new grain and their new wine proved abundant.—Back on the land, this seasonal rejoicing sometimes degenerated into sexual license, as can be seen from Hos 4:10–12; 7:14; 9:1–2 in the Jewish Publication Society's English translation of *The Propehts,* Philadelphia 1978, with the pertinent footnotes.

3. The Pilgrimage-Feast of Booths, Deut 16:13–15

(13) After the ingathering from your threshing floor and your vat, you shall hold a [77] Pilgrimage-Feast of Booths for seven days.

(14) You shall rejoice on your pilgrimage-feast, with your son and daughter, your male and female slave, and the Levite, the stranger, the fatherless and the widow in your communities.

(15) You shall observe the pilgrimage-festival for your God YHWH seven days, in the place that YHWH will choose; for your God YHWH will bless all[78] your crops and all your undertakings, and you shall truly have joy.

Comment. The "ingathering ... from the vat" is mentioned because the new wine, after being trodden out in the winepress and running down into the vat, is not left there (where it will spoil) but emptied into jars and put away in a suitable storage place. The legislator evidently contemplates a season when the pressure of farm work is relatively light, so that a festive period of seven days is practicable. He makes the temple visit that long because he wants it to be an occasion for thanksgiving for all the gifts of the land. It is because a sojourn of seven days requires some sort of housing that he changes the old name of the pilgrimage from the Pilgrimage of Ingathering to the Pilgrimage of Booths—no doubt booths made of leafy branches (Neh 8:15; cf. Isa 1:8; Job 27:18), probably for shelter from the heat of the day as well as for sleeping in; cf. Jonah 4:5. Again we do not know whether he let every family choose the seven days most convenient for it or contemplated an advance notice by some sort of authority. —The prohibition of Exod 23:19b, originally applicable, according to our surmise *ad loc.,* to autumn pilgrimage sacrifices, is generalized by D and transferred to the end of the dietary laws, Deut 14:21b. [The jars into which the wine was emptied from the vat no doubt had lids.]

---

[77] Read *skwt* on the analogy of *šb'wt* in v. 10. MT is due to contamination by *hskwt* in v. 16. If the author had written *hskwt,* he would, in accordance with the rule for a direct object determined by the definite article in prose, have written *'t hg hskwt.*

[78] Lit. "you in all."

4. The Conclusion, Deut 16:16–17

(16) Three times a year—at the Pilgrimage of Unleavened Bread, at the Pilgrimage of Weeks, and at the Pilgrimage of Booths—all your males shall appear before your God YHWH in the place that he will choose. None shall appear before YHWH empty-handed (17) but each with his own gift, according to the blessing that your God YHWh has bestowed upon you.

Comment.   It has already been explained that according to 16:1 ff. the Pilgrimage of Unleavened Bread takes place on the first night of the seven days, and why. Vv. 16b–17 seem to imply, like v. 10, that money gifts are also acceptable; but in the case of the Pilgrimage of Unleavened Bread, the passover offering is evidently indispensable.

VI. The Second Ritual Decalogue, Exod 34:19–27

Preliminary, vv. 1–9

After going up to the Mount of God at YHWH's behest, and leaving Joshua at the foot of it and Aaron and Hur (Hur was already associated with Aaron in 17:10, 12) in the camp in charge of the people, Moses stays at the top forty days and nights to receive the slabs of stone on which YHWH has inscribed "the teaching and commandments" which he has written for the people's instruction (Exod 24:12–15a,18b E). The people, however, grow impatient with waiting and press Aaron to make a "god" to lead them. Aaron demands whatever earrings they have, encloses them in a mold (*ḥéreṭ*) of some sort, and produces a calf of cast gold. The people hail it as the god "who brought you up from Egypt." Aaron builds an altar before it and proclaims a pilgrimage to the altar—in honor of YHWH, to be sure—for the following day. The people come, feast, and arise to dance (Exod 32:1–10 E). Though sundry retarding episodes are included (the untangling of which will be attempted in Chapter VIII), we read, in 32:7—33:23, that Moses descends with the two tablets, but on seeing the people disporting themselves before the calf hurls the tablets to the ground and smashes them; and YHWH orders Moses to lead the people to the Promised Land with YHWH's angel going before them but with YHWH absent from their midst. Moses begs to be informed, at least, of YHWH's attributes, so that he may know how to appease him when necessary. YHWH now tries to compromise by promisng that his own presence (*panim*) will march ahead, but Moses insists that YHWH's marching in the midst of the people is the minimum without which he would rather not budge from where they are. YHWH apparently yields, and also agrees to reveal his graciousness and compassion to Moses at a spot "on the rock" (33:22).—Ch. 34 then begins with YHWH ordering Moses to carve out two slabs of stone like the first pair—according to 34:1b, for YHWH himself to rewrite *the contents of the first ones* on. Moses prepares the stones and takes them up on the mountain early the following morning. YHWH descends in a cloud (6ab) "and YHWH proclaimed: YHWH, a God compassionate and gracious, (7) extending kindness to the thousandth generation, forgiving iniquity, transgression, and sin; yet not remitting all punishment but visiting the iniquity of fathers upon children and children's children, upon the third and fourth generations."

(8–9) Moses quickly bows in reverence, but the announcement of YHWH's quality of forgiveness emboldens him to request, again,

(9) "If I have gained Your favor, my Lord, pray, let my Lord march among us, even though this is a stiffnecked people. Pardon our iniquity and our sin, and take us for Your own." This was originally followed by v.28, and vv. 10–27 are an interpolation, as has already been pointed out.[79]

(10–27) YHWH responds with a covenant, to replace the one that Israel forfeited (as evidenced by Moses' smashing of the first tablets). It is modeled on the ten ritual laws of Exod 23—vv. 10–11, 12, 13b, 15, 16a, 16b, 18a, 18b, 19a, 19b—which represent Israel's obligations, and also (though indirectly) on the promise of a safe journey to the Promised Land and a prosperous occupation of it (23:20–33), which are YHWH's obligation but are accompanied by a warning. In the present passage, YHWH's promise and warning come first, because they are a suitable preface to the obligation of Israel which here heads the list: (17) "You shall not make molten gods for yourself." In the circumstances, this is more timely (and in any case more practical and practicable) than 23:13b ("Make no mention of other gods; they shall not be heard on your lips").

---

[79] See above, n. 62.

As for YHWH's introductory promise and warning (34:11–16), that is modeled not directly on 23:20–33 but on the first five verses of D's modification of the latter in Deut 7. For in addition to eliminating the role of the angel (like Deut 7:1–2), it substitutes for the pillars of Exod 23:24 the triad altars-pillars-sacred posts (Heb. *'ašerim,* 34:13), which is only one link short of Deut 7:5's tetrad altars-pillars-sacred posts-carved images; and not only is this tetrad characteristic of Deuteronomy, since it occurs again in Deut 12:3, but the only remaining example of a "sacred post" (*'ašera*) in the Pentateuch likewise occurs in Deuteronomy (16:21). Moreover, Exod 34:13 further agrees with Deut 7:5 in being formulated in the second person plural in the midst of a patch of second person singulars. And still the Deuteronomic influences in our document are not exhausted. There is, of course, Exod 34:24, of which even those who minimize the Deuteronomic coloring of our source admit that it presupposes a centralized cult. For v.23 is, just like the beginning of Deut 16:16, borrowed from Exod 23:17; and where Deuteronomy betrays its special concern by adding the words "in the place that he will choose," our passage does the same by adding a whole verse (Exod 34:24): "For though I will drive out nations from your path and enlarge your territory, no one will covet your territory when you go up to appear before your God YHWH three times a year." Naturally, a border area whose able-bodied adult males are all concentrated at a shrine is only liable to become an irresistible temptation to the neighbors on the other side of the border if that shrine is situated a great distance away, not if it is within the border area in question and within easy reach of every part of that area.

And there is still more. Exod 23:10 is not taken over, because Deuteronomy has abolished the ritual law of the fallow year (and has substituted for it the social law of the debt remission year, Deut 15:1–11); and just as, so we have seen, Deut 16 deliberately abolishes the pilgrimage of the seventh day of the week of unleavened bread, so our author rewords Exod 23:18 in such a way that both its halves refer to the one passover sacrifice (34:25), even coining in 34:25b the phrase *zébah hag happásah* "the passover pilgrimage sacrifice," which strikes us as odd but accords completely with what we have seen to be the import of Deut 16:1–8. And in the circumstances, the fact that our friend has substituted the expression *labbóqer* of Deut 16:4b for Exod 23:18b's *'ad bóqer* is not devoid of significance. It is, then, in order to compensate for these two Deuteronomy-inspired omissions that our author has (1) borrowed his Exod 34:19–20a from the E passage Exod 13:12–13 (the laws governing the male firstborn of domestic horned livestock, asses, and human beings) and (2) deliberately placed the clause "and none shall appear before me emptyhanded," which in Exod 23 stands at the end of v.15 and is merely part of the commandment to observe the Pilgrimage of Unleavened Bread, in a new position, at the end of 34:20, for no other reason than that there, standing between the commandments about the firstborn and the sabbath and incapable of combining with either, it must necessarily count as a separate commandment. Thus the "ritual decalogue" of Exod 34 comprises the following items:

I, v.17, Prohibition of molten gods.

II, v.18, The Pilgrimage of Unleavened Bread.

III, vv.19–20ba. How to deal with the various categories of male firstborn that are YHWH's.

IV, v.20bb. None shall appear before YHWH empty-handed.

V. v.21. The Sabbath.

VI. v.22a. A Pilgrimage of Weeks.

VII. v.22b. The Pilgrimage of Ingathering.

VIII. v.25. An addendum to II: two rules governing the passover, which has become, as in D, the pilgrimage sacrifice of the Pilgrimage of Unleavened Bread.

IX, 26a. An explication of VI.

X, 26b. An addendum to VII: a practice to be avoided by those who make the season of Ingathering an occasion for disposing of their remaining surplus male kids. (Cf. in ch. IV *ad fin.* the explanation of the bearing of Precept X of E's decalogue on Precept VI thereof.)

Because our interpolator is strongly influenced by D, we shall assign to him the siglum X[D]. It must not be supposed, however, that X[D] agrees with D one hundred per cent; he is a Deuteronomist but a dissident one. Firstly, in 34:22a he accepts D's "*a* pilgrimage of weeks" instead of the original "*the* Pilgrimage of the Grain Harvest" of Exod 23:16a, but he objects to D's dissociating it from the bringing of first fruits: first fruits must be brought on this pilgrimage; and since now wheat as well as barley is available, the first fruits must, as a matter of reverence, be brought from wheat, the more valuable crop. And secondly, since the original date of the third pilgrimage, "the beginning of the year" (Exod 23:16b), is now too close to the second, X[D] requires that the two months of ingathering be moved from the beginning to the end of the year and that the Pilgrimage of Ingathering be observed at the end of the ingathering season, which is now the end of the year. Since, however, he neither adopts D's new name for it ("Pilgrimage of Booths") nor requires any booths, he evidently intends the Pilgrimage of Ingathering to fall on the very last day of the year (*tqupat hassana*) and to last only one day, 34:22b. Since there were thus two opinions on the subject, it would seem that Neh 8:13 ff. preserves a historical recollection that the observance of seven days of dwelling in booths was not firmly established until the Persian period. Since its origin is Deut 16:13–15, which is from all appearances Proto-Deuteronomic, its triumph is the triumph of an element of Israelian heritage in Judaism.

What these three tables have in common are exact datings according to the numbered-month calendar (first month . . . seventh month). The earliest reasonably datable examples of the use of this calendar are: (1) II Ki 25, covering 588–560 B.C.E.; (2) the Book of Jeremiah, which includes a few such dates from 604 (Jer 36:9) to 586 B.C.E.; and (3) the Book of Ezekiel, containing such dates from 593 to 571 B.C.E. There is of course also I Ki 12:31, which tells of a pilgrimage of the fifteenth day of the eighth month that was instituted at Bethel by Jeroboam I (end of 10th century B.C.E.); but that is part of a wild legend, teeming with improbabilities and anachronisms, that couldn't have arisen before the event it concludes with, namely Josiah's desecration of the altar of Bethel (II Ki 23:15–18). Now, this calendar, of such late attestation, bears a striking resemblance to the Babylonian one, its "first month" corresponding to Nisan, the month with which the new year began in Babylon; and indeed already Nehemiah in his memoirs uses none but the actual Babylonian names of the months; cf. also Esther, I Maccabees, and ever after. It is therefore natural to suspect that the numbered-months adaptation of the Babylonian calendar only came into use during the long reign of Manasseh, a submissive vassal of Assyria. I sensed confirmation that the old native month-names had not entirely fallen out of use even in the last years of the kingdom of Judah's existence when, in 1940, Torczyner (later Tur-Sinai), published a pocket edition of the Lachish ostraca,[80] including three that had been discovered in

---

[80] H. Torczyner, *The Lachish Ostraca, Letters of the Time of Jeremiah* (The Library of Palestinology of The Jewish Palestine Exploration Society, ed. by S. Yeivin, XV–XVII), Jerusalem 1940 (according to the English title-page of the Hebrew work).

1938, after the publication that year, in English, of the ostraca found in 1935. For one of these new texts, a fragmentary one published in the Hebrew edition as no. 20, begins with the word *btš'yt,* which the editor rightly interpreted to mean "In the ninth (scil. year of King Zedekiah)" followed by three further characters and a break. This the editor read and restored *byw/m* 'on the day,' but I insisted[81] that on graphic grounds alone[82] the third sign in the second word could only be a *resh* and the reading must therefore be *byr/ḥ* 'in the month of,' and that the month-name in question must be assumed to have been a native Hebrew (or Phoenician) proper name, like those which follow *yéraḥ* in I Ki 6:37, 38; 8:2, i.e. not an ordinal number like those which follow *ḥódeš* until they are displaced by the Babylonian names Nisan, Iyyar, etc. (In I Ki 6:1 the words *zw hw' ḥdš,* wanting in the Septuagint, are evidently a gloss constructed on the basis of v.37.)[83]

The foregoing ought to be of some asistance to readers in overcoming a perhaps natural inner resistance to the evidence that will be presented below in support of the view that not only Ezek 45:18 ff. (of course!) but also Lev 23 and Num 28–29 postdate both D and X[D]. [On the Manassean date of the adoption of the numbered-months calendar, see the Addenda.]

---

[81] In BASOR 80 (1940), 12–13. I don't think my view has ever been seriously disputed.

[82] Apart from the fact that in the Lachish ostraca as in the Siloam inscription—to which may now be added the Arad ostraca—the word for *day* is written not *ywm* but *ym,* and was evidently pronounced not *yom* but *yam* (cf. the plural forms *yamim, yme, ymot*) in all of documented preexilic Judah.

[83] Of course my reading and interpretation of the critical word in Lachish 20 would be brilliantly confirmed by the Arad inscription on which the late Yohonon Aharoni read *bšlšt yrh ṣh* "in the third (year), month of ṣh" if the reading *yrh ṣh* were assured; but it is disputed orally by Aharoni's collaborator Yosef Naveh. The Arad inscriptions are published in Yohonon Aharoni, *Arad Inscriptions,* Jerusalem 1975 (folio), with a contribution by Yosef Naveh and Tiberian vocalization of the transcriptions by Hayyim Etan. [The other inscriptions found in the latest preexilic stratum of Arad are official orders (presumably from outside Arad) to an *official* or officer stationed at Arad. That they employ the numbered-months calendar is no surprise, since we have seen that there can be no doubt about its being current in the southern kingdom during the last decades of its existence.]

1. Lev 23:4-44

As is well known, Lev 17-26(27) is, broadly speaking, the source H. Within Lev 23:4-44, however, only vv.9-32 and 39-43 retain the pure style of H, which is somewhat less drab than that of the corresponding part of P, while other paragraphs are more or less assimilated to the typical P style.

(a) The season of ingathering

We shall deal first with vv.39-43, which parallel the more normalized verses 33-36 but exhibit the word *šabbaton* which is characteristic of H in this chapter. On close examination, the words "on the fifteenth day of the seventh month" in v.39 seem to be secondary, since after such an exact date (1) the further specification "when you gather/have gathered in the yield of your land" is superfluous and (2) the conclusion 41b*b,* "you shall observe it in the seventh month," diminishes the specificity of the opening instead of adding to it. I therefore conclude that originally v.39 lacked the words "on the fifteenth day of the seventh month" and simply began thus: "Mark, when you gather in the yield of your land, etc.," in other words, that *its starting point is Exod 34:22b,* and what it adds to it is first of all the extension of the duration of the pilgrimage from Exod 34:22b's last day of the year to its last seven days, to that extent bringing it into conformity with Deut 16:13, 15 over the opposition of X^D. Being the last seven days in the year, they are naturally followed immediately by the first new moon of the following year, which was no doubt "commemorated with loud blasts" in the manner of the later new moon of the seventh month, Lev 23:23, since it was shown further back (in ch. IV) that according to Ps 81:4 the earlier "first new moon of the year," at the beginning of the season of ingathering, was celebrated in just that manner in early "Joseph." And in my opinion, it is what we have seen to be the situation contemplated by Lev 23:39 (minus the later addition "on the fifteenth day of the seventh month" at its beginning), in which the *seven days* of the pilgrimage of ingathering *were immediately followed by the first new moon of a new year,* that accounts for the paradox that our verse, after ordaining a pilgrimage lasting only *seven* days in all, goes on to prescribe, in addition to a complete rest (*šabbaton*) on the first day, a complete rest on the *eighth* day.

For the seven days of the pilgrimage proper, H further accepts D's precept of rejoicing and, moreover, explicates the manner of such rejoicing as follows: (4) "On the first day, get yourselves branches[84] of handsome trees[85]—palm branches and boughs of leafy trees and wadi willows—and rejoice before your God YHWH seven days." V.41 then repeats that the pilgrimage celebrations are to continue for seven days and adds that in terms of the new, numbered-months, calendar the month in which—i.e. at whose end—this is to be done is the seventh month, which explanation, we have already observed, was added at the end of v.41 *before the* final *change,* that *of beginning the seven days on the fifteenth of the month, was added at the beginning of v.39.* Finally, as an afterthought, the Deuteronomic principle of dwelling in booths during those seven days is added in v.42, which has apparently (by haplography) lost a *w* at the beginning after the *w* at the end of v.41; and a curious reason is appended in v.43, thus: (42) "[And] you shall live in booths seven days—all citizens in Israel shall live in booths—(43) in order that you may recall, throughout the ages, that I had the Israelite people live in booths when I brought them out of the land of Egypt, I your God YHWH." Just what the author means by "booths" (*sukkot*) in v.43 is not self-evident to me. Is it inexact for

---

[84] On this meaning of *pri* see in English *Hebrew and Semitic Studies Presented to G.R. Driver,* Oxford 1963, pp. 72-76, or in Hebrew *Henoch Yalon Jubilee Volume,* Jerusalem 1963, pp. 167-170.

[85] Because *pry 'ṣ hdr* is followed (not by *wkpt tmrym* but) by *kpt tmrym,* I do not take the former as a specific category of branches but as a generic expression which the following ones explicate. The text of course means that the branches are to be carried and waved festively, not to be used for building booths as in Neh 8:15.

tents, or did the writer, like Rabbi Eliezer in the Mekilta on Exod
12:37, understand the *sukkot* which was the Israelites' first station
on their exodus from Egypt to be not the proper name of a place
but literal booths?

But the priests of Judah, who retained such an accurate memory
of the original character of the passover sacrifice and meal as they
give evidence of in Exod 12:1–11, 46, evidently retained a no less
accurate recollection of the original dates and manners of observance of the autumn great new moon and the autumn pilgrimage
that we were able to reconstruct further back (in ch. IV) with the
help of the Gezer Calendar and Ps 81. For in the month of the new,
numbered-months, calendar, the seventh month, which they
adopted for both of these festivals, they eventually prescribed
"complete rest, a sacred occasion commemorated with loud
blasts" for the first day (Lev 23:23) and ordained that the Pilgrimage of Booths begin with the *fifteenth,* or *full moon* (Lev 23:33–36).
But while—in moving the latter up from the last seven days where
they originally had them—they have them now continue for seven
days starting with the fifteenth of the month, they also carry along
the extra eighth day; and whereas in vv.39 ff. this extra day is due
to its beginning a new year, it now, in v.36, appears as an *'ǎṣéret*
which hangs in the air. I explained above, on Deut 16:8, that this
word means 'concluding solemnity,' and such is evidently also the
opinion of the Septuagint, which renders it everywhere by *exodion,*
meaning 'a marching out, or finale.' [The Rabbis evidently likewise
understood it thus, for they regularly refer to the second of the
three Pilgrimage Festivals not as *Šabu'ot* 'Weeks' but as *'Aṣéret*
"Concluding Solemnity," to which they only exceptionally add
šellappésaḥ 'of the Passover (as the Season of Unleavened Bread had
come be called).'[86] So, too, Josephus, Antiq. III 10:6, testifies that

---

[86] Hereby hangs a fascinating tale. Masseket Soferim 18:3 end prescribes for *ḥag haššabu'ot*
recitation, by the Levitical singers, of Ps 29. The reason is obvious: the psalm's majestic
description of a storm traveling inland from the Mediterranean to the desert, with YHWH in
its midst uttering peals of thunder and flashing darts of lightning, is reminiscent of the ter-

the Hebrews call Pentecost (in Aramaic, of course) *Asartha.*]

Bold though it is, the above explanation of the origin of the "concluding solemnity" to the Pilgrimage of Booths can only be given up in favor of a convincing alternative.

(b) The season of the grain harvest

Even more remarkable than the two sections of Lev 23 relating to the season of ingathering is the one large section, vv.9–22, relating to the season of the grain harvest. For one thing, it abolishes the grain harvest pilgrimage altogether; not only does it avoid the use of the word *ḥag* 'pilgrimage-festival'—and that this omission is not accidental is confirmed by the absence of the term from the corresponding section of Num 28–29, namely Num 28:26–31— but it rules very clearly and emphatically (in v. 21) that the day of Pentecost is to be, for all time, a sacred occasion on which "you shall not work at your occupations *in all your settlements."* Moreover, in addition to being so embracing that it includes even the social laws relating to the harvest season (i.e. v.22, a combination of Lev 19:9 and 10b, with 10a omitted because it refers not to the grain harvest but to the vintage), our pericope is not content, as are vv. 8, 24, 27, 36a, 36b, to declare that communal offerings by fire are due without specifying what they are: in this case, we are told just what must be offered, vv.16b–20, and the communal communion sacrifices of v.19b are exceptional.[87]

---

rifying theophany on Sinai at the giving of the Law, which according to Rabbinic reckoning took place on the sixth of Sivan, the Pharisaic date of Pentecost; see Mekilta on Exod 19:1–5. (Unfortunately, Lauterbach in his English translation of the Jewish Publication Society's edition of the Mekilta carelessly printed at vv. 10, 11, and 15 "the fourth/fifth/sixth day of the *week"* instead of *"month,"* but Pseudo-Jonathan on v. 16 has rightly *bšyt' byrḥ'* and Rashi on v. 11 has *šsh bḥdš.*) In contrast, the words *exodiou skēnēs* which the Septuagint adds to the caption of Ps 29 are a puzzle. Surely the word *skēnēs* was added—perhaps not even already in the Hebrew original but only in the Greek translation—by somebody (an Alexandrian Jew?) who knew only the biblical names of the festivals. For *exodiou* alone would reflect a Hebrew *la'ăṣéret,* meaning, *in Rabbinic terminology,* "for Pentecost."

[87] Num 29:39 surely enumerates various kinds of *individual* sacrifices that may be offered, but "the Ezekielian utopia" of Ezek 45:15–18 suggests the survival of at least the idea of

But it is not only at the end of the grain harvest season that our table of laws contains surprises. Special ceremonies are also prescribed for the beginning of the seven weeks that are counted off from the beginning of the grain harvest, Lev 23:9–16a. D's interposition of seven weeks between the beginning of the harvest and its celebration, accepted by X[D], is also accepted by H, of course, since it is a consequence of the centralization of the cult, as was explained in connection with Deut 16:9, and this principle of D was accepted by all its successors. But H's priestly mind felt a need for some token presentation of first fruits to the Deity before men might partake of the new crop, and so he devised for the very beginning of the harvest the ceremony of vv. 9 ff., in which the first *'ómer* of grain reaped anywhere in the country is formally presented at the Temple on behalf of the community, thereby making the use of the crop permissible to everybody everywhere; and it is on the day on which this is done that the counting of seven weeks to the actual holy day of first fruits is begun. Obvious exegetical problems are (1) the nature and the implications of the expression "on the morrow of the sabbath" in vv. 11 and 15, (2) the quantity to be reaped, and (3) the manner in which it is to be presented. The normative halakah on these points is considerably removed from the peshaṭ, and so we merely refer to Mishnah Menaḥot X—which is printed as chapter VI in the Babylonian Talmud—and to the baraitot cited in the Babylonian Talmud (alternatively, to the baraitot printed as Parashah X of Emor in the Venice 5305 edition of the Sifra [reprinted by offset, Berlin 5685], cols. 199–202). They include the interpretation of the word *'ómer,* after Exod 16:36, as one-tenth of an ephah (of hulled grain). I do not, however, accept even the current translation of *'ómer* as "sheaf," but only "armful,"[88] and I also correct the current rendering of *tnupa* from "waving" to "designation" (scil. as YHWH's).[89]

---

several communal communion sacrifices. (Exod 24:5, of course, likewise speaks of sacrifices on behalf of the people to be partaken of by the "youths" who represent it.)

[88] Following G. Dalman, *Arbeit und Sitte in Palästina* III, pp. 18, 46 ff., 49 ff., 52, 58, 62 ff.

[89] Following J. Milgrom, IEJ 22 (1972), pp. 33–38. (The word means literally 'elevation.')

As for *mimmohŏrat haššabbat* in vv. 11 and 15a, I claim that in both
these verses it is a gloss, not only because it fits awkwardly into the
two sentences in question, as is particularly the case in v.15a, but
also because in both these cases it must designate a day, whereas
the word *šabbat* in vv. 15b and 16 can only mean *week,* even in the
identical sequence *mimmohŏrat haššabbat.* For v.16a must be translated: "you shall count until the day after the seventh *week*—fifty
days," since it does not begin to deal with anything different from
the end of v.15 but merely explicates the last two words of v.15,
which do begin a new sentence, "They must be complete";[90] and
this cannot very well be said of sabbaths, but only of weeks. It follows that in vv. 11 and 15 "the day after the sabbath" is a gloss.
Here is a translation of Lev 23:9–21 that will, among other things,
bring out this fact as well as the insights that have already been
gained above:

(9) YHWH spoke to Moses as follows: (10) Speak to the Israelite
people and say to them: When you enter the land which I am giving to
you and you reap its harvest, you shall bring the first armful of your
harvest to the priest (11) for designation as YHWH's, and the priest
shall so designate it (on the day after the sabbath) for acceptance on
your behalf. (12) On the day that you designate the armful, you shall
offer as burnt offering to YHWH a lamb, without blemish, in its first
year. (13) The accompanying meal offering shall consist of two tenths-
of-an-ephah of semolina[91] with oil mixed in—an offering by fire of
pleasing odor to YHWH—while the accompanying libation shall consist of a quarter of a hin of wine. (14) Until that day, until you have
brought the offering to your God, do not partake [from the new crop]

[90] That a new clause begins with *tmymt,* so that the following word *thyynh* does not need to
be juggled away in the translation, was not yet realized by The Jewish Publication Society's
new translation of *The Torah* in its first edition of 1962; this insight is first reflected in the
Revised Edition of 1967.

[91] This is notoriously the exact equivalent of the Hebrew *sólet*; see G. Dalman, *Arbeit und
Sitte in Palästina,* III, pp. 292–294; and since the context is not poetry but in the nature of a
recipe, the weasel words "choice flour" of the new Jewish Publication Society translation of
The Torah and The Prophets are to be deprecated rather than commended.

of any bread or parched or fresh grain[91a]—a law for all time, through the ages, in all your settlements.

(15) And from the day (on the day after the sabbath) on which you present the armful for designation, you shall count off seven weeks. They must be complete: (16) you must count until the day after the seventh week—fifty days. Then you shall present a tribute from the new crop[92] to YHWH:

(17) you shall bring from your settlements two [loaves of] bread, comprising two tenths-of-an-ephah of semolina and baked after leavening, for designation as the first fruits for YHWH.

(18) With the bread you shall offer, as burnt offerings to YHWH, seven yearling lambs without blemish, one young bull of the herd, and two rams (with their meal offerings and libations), an offering by fire of pleasing odor to YHWH.

(19) You shall also offer one he-goat as a purgation offering and two yearly lambs as a sacrifice of communion.

(20) These two lambs the priest shall designate as YHWH's in his presence, together with the bread of first fruits; they shall be holy to YHWH for the priest.

(21) And on that very day you shall proclaim a solemnity.[93] It shall be holy to you; you shall not work at your occupations—a law for all time, in all your settlements, throughout the ages.

But if the secondary character of the phrase "on the day after the sabbath" in vv. 11 and 15 is certain, it is by no means equally certain that the author of the pericope did not in fact intend the designation ceremony to be performed, and the counting off of the seven weeks to be begun, on a Sunday. For the word he uses for 'week' in 15b–16 is not the usual word *šabua'* but *šabbat,* and there

---

[91a] Or perhaps: of any cereal [Isa 28:28], parched or fresh.

[92] Of wheat, as is implied by the word *semolina* in the next verse. Cf. *The American Heritage Dictionary*'s definition of semolina as "the gritty, coarse particles *of wheat* (my italics) left after the finer flour has passed through the bolting machine" (the modern descendant of the *napa* of Mishnah Abot 5:15).

[93] Ending the sentence here results in the same phrase as is present in Isa 1:13 (where, by the way, as in Ps 101:5, it is necessary to emend *'ukal* to *'akil,* cf. Jer 6:11; 10:10 [last clause]; Joel 2:11; Amos 7:10).

is reason to believe that when this word is used in the sense of week
it means specifically a sabbatical week. This is suggested (1) by its
etymology; (2) by the fact that in the other case where it occurs—
namely in Lev 25:8 (bis), where it is likewise a question of counting
off, though in this case of counting off weeks of years—there can be
no doubt but sabbatical weeks are meant, i.e. heptads of years in
each of which the seventh is a sabbatical year (*šnat šabbaton*, v.5);
and (3) by the peculiar state of affairs in Num 28 (P). For here (a)
there is nothing at all corresponding to the paragraph Lev
23:9–16a, which makes one suspect that the author was anxious to
avoid any use in this connection of the word *šabbat* in either of its
senses; and (b) Num 28:26–31, corresponding to Lev 23:16b–21,
begins with the words, "And on the Day of First Fruits, when you
present a tribute from the new crop,[94] to YHWH, at (the conclusion of) your (counting of) weeks (*šabu'ot*) . . ." It further diverges
from the Lev 23 parallel not only by not specifying either the
quantity of cereal that goes into the "tribute from the new crop" or
the fact that it takes the form of semolina for the accompanying
two lambs of communal sacrifice of communion (though it may be
relying on Lev 23 for these particulars), and it also prescribes two
young bulls and one ram (instead of the 1 bull and 2 rams of Lev
23:18) for burnt offering: but these divergences seem to me less
significant than the fact that Num 28:26 expresses the notion of
'weeks' not by *šabbatot* but by *šabu'ot*. Since P retained H's "tribute
from the new crop ceremony," he doubtless also retained H's
"Armful for Designation" ceremony despite his silence about it;
but if it became objectively practicable to hold it on a Monday, he
did not wish to have it, and the beginning of the counting off, put
off for six days until Sunday.

The H and P regulations pertaining to the harvest are not only
elaborate but also mutually contradictory. We called attention
above to the fact that Lev 23 employs for "week" the Hebrew word

---

[94] See above, n. 92.

šabbat which, we saw reasons to believe, means specifically "sabbat-ical week," and that glosses have been added in Lev 23:11 and 15 to make sure that the counting off will be begun on a Sunday, whereas Num 28:34 ff. deliberately suppresses the word šabbat and features šabua' so as to obviate the implication that the counting off must start on a Sunday. What with the complexity and the incon-sistency, it is no wonder that those laws have been a subject of dis-pute among the sects from antiquity down to the present day. It was natural that the Pharisaic-Rabbinic interpretation of "on the day after the sabbath" as meaning "on the day after the first yom ṭob (biblical miqra qódeš, Lev 23:7, 8b) of Pésaḥ (as the week of maṣṣot has been called in Judaism since tannaitic times) was rejected both by the Jubilees-Qumran school and the Boethusians in antiquity and by Karaism since the Middle Ages. (A remnant of the latter, which survives in the state of Israel, maintains that the counting off must start on a Sunday, not only in years when it does so among the Rabbanites but every year.) At the same time, all the deviant forms of Judaism share with the mainstream the assumption that the grain harvest pentecontad must be charted in relation to some landmark in the week of unleavened bread, which is hardly the intention of H and P. The pertinent legislation of these codes derives ultimately from Exod 23:16a in the Israelian document E, by way of Deut 16:8-11 in the likewise Israelian document D and of Exod 34:22a in the document X^D, which whatever its national-ity, was profoundly influenced by the Israelian document D (as was demonstrated in Chapter VI). Since these passages are all oriented by the—locally and annually variable—day of the beginning of the grain harvest, it is probable that H likewise meant to let nature take its course, without reference to the week of unleavened bread. However, the shifting of the beginning of the latter from "the new moon of milky grain" to the full moon of the first month of the numbered-months calendar (see immediately below) brought it down to a point in the course of the natural year when fully ripe barley has appeared in some areas of the country, which led later generations to look for a landmark defined by the festival week.

But obviously, in the last analysis the Jewish *Sefirah* (counting off) and Shabu'ot (or, in the rabbinic idiom, 'Aṣéret) are part of Judaism's Israelian heritage.

(c) Passover and unleavened bread:

Still to be studied are the H and P paragraphs on the passover offering and the seven days of unleavened bread: Lev 23:5–8 and Num 28:16–25. They both agree that the passover sacrifice is to be offered "between the evenings"[95] on the day before the pilgrimage of unleavened bread, that the first and seventh days of the week of unleavened bread are to be sacred occasions on which no work may be done, and that public offerings by fire are to be presented on each of the seven days, with the difference that P specifies what they are to consist of. According to both, the passover is to be offered on the fourteenth day of the first month, and the pilgrimage of the first day of unleavened bread falls on the fifteenth day. Now, we can guess why the passover sacrifice, which D and X[D] had dated at sunset just inside the week of unleavened bread, was moved back by H and P to the afternoon of the preceding day, as in the days before the centralization of the cult. It was presumably because, according to P, a man can be prevented from visiting the Temple not only by absence on a distant journey (a contingency D never considered) but also by ritual impurity owing to contact with the dead, Num 9:9–14; for P requires a full seven days for purification from this particular impurity, Num 19, especially vv. 11 ff. (D perhaps required merely a ritual bath, washing one's clothes, and waiting until sunset.) P's view was therefore that neither distance nor impurity excused a person from abstaining from anything

---

[95] Though most moderns prefer to interpret this expression to mean "at twilight," there is something to be said for the rabbinic view that it means in the afternoon. The shortness of the subtropical twilight, even in spring and in summer, may strike a visitor to Israel from New York, let alone one from Chicago, London or Oxford.

leavened during the unleavened season, but that they did excuse him from coming to the Temple or even having the passover offered for him in the Temple by a friend or relative and partaking of it outside. (Later sources contemplate relaxations; see II Chron 30:17-20; Mishnah Pesaḥim 7:6.)

Another problem is the shifting of the date from the new moon to the full moon. If, however, our above explanation of the ultimate fixing of the beginning of the Pilgrimage of Booths at the full moon of the seventh month is accepted, the fixing of the date of the Pilgrimage of Unleavened Bread on the fifteenth day of the first month must have been dictated by a desire for symmetry, with exactly two pilgrimages a year exactly six months apart. (That the priestly sources do not require any pilgrimage in connection with the grain harvest has been amply demonstrated.) Any reluctance to recognize the operation of a striving for symmetry should be lessened by a scrutiny of the fragment of utopian legislation Ezek 45:18-25, which requires a semi-annual temple purgation day on the first days of the first and seventh months and a semi-annual pilgrimage in the middle of each of those two months. For, despite Zimmerli, the Septuagint's reading "in the seventh month" must be adopted in v.20, since if v.20 as well as v.18 were speaking about the first month v.21 would begin not with "in the first month on the fourteenth day of the month," but with "and on the fourteenth day of the same (first) month"; cf. Lev 23:6, 27, 34; Num 29:7, 12.

(d) Some other late features of H and P

Recalling that H and P postdate D and X^D will make it easier to understand the inclusion in Lev 19:4(H) of an adaptation of X^D's "You shall make no molten gods for yourself" (Exod 34:17) and the penetration of the originally, it would seem, E-D expression "a land flowing with milk and honey" into H (Lev 20:24) and Ezekiel (Ezek 20:6,15) among other authors, as also the fact that the

Hosea-Deuteronomy triad new grain-new wine-new oil (with the
three items named in nature's own order) reappears in Num 18:12
but in the opposite order. [See the discussion in n. 136.]

Another problem that becomes easier to solve when it is realized
that H and P postdate D are the many anomalies in the H or P
counterpart—Lev 26:33b ff.—of D's "vassalage treaty," Deut 28. It
is true that the threatening part of the D chapter, vv.15-68, was
hardly composed in a single breath, but it remains true to form. A
suzerain would be defeating his purpose of deterring his vassal
from playing him false if he weakened at any point and intimated
that his bark was worse than his bite and the vassal need never
despair of being restored to grace even if he rebels and fails; and
by the same token, a religious writer who wished to deter Israel
from going the limit would be defeating his own ends if he assured
Israel that YHWH was incurably indulgent after all. It is only after
Israel has gone the limit, as proved by the fact that its state has
been destroyed and much of its population exiled, that Deuteronomy comes up with Deut 30:1-10 (Deut 28:49—30:20 is the *later*
conclusion to Deuteronomy), assuring Israel that, if it will but turn
back to YHWH with all its heart and soul, YHWH will not only
take it back into favor and restore it to its land but will even give it
a more obedient nature so as to insure it against a repetition of the
disaster. So too it is in the post-disaster later introduction to
Deuteronomy (the earlier one begins at 4:44) that we read verses
holding out a promise of repentance and forgiveness (4:29-31). Is
not, then, the confusion in Lev 26:33b ff. to be accounted for by an
analogous evolution? Tentatively, I would make vv.37b-38,46 the
original continuation of v.33a. Then, after at least the first deporta-
tion from Judah in 597, there will have been added vv.39-40a,
44-45: (39) "Those of you who survive shall be heartsick over their
iniquity[96] in the land of your enemies; more, they shall be heartsick

---

[96] If the meaning of v. 39 is, as is usually supposed, merely that the survivors shall "pine
away because of their iniquity," what is the implication of v.38? Is it that the exiles of v. 38
will perish because of their blamelessness? Surely, the thing to do is to look for some mean-

over the iniquities of their fathers; (40) and they shall confess their iniquity and the iniquity of their fathers . . . (44) But even then, when they are in the land of their enemies, I will not have rejected or spurned them so as to destroy them, annulling my covenant with them; for I YHWH am their God. (45) And I will remember in their favor the covenant with the ancients whom I freed from Egypt in the sight of the nations to be their God, I YHWH." (Cf. Ezek 20:9,14,22; since it was in the sight of the nations that YHWH freed the Israelites from Egypt to be their God, it would be a profanation of his name if he ceased to be their God.)

As for the remaining added verses—33b-37, 40b-43—they express (in what chronological order, I have not been able to determine) the following ideas: The purpose of the desolation of the land is that it may *atone* for the sabbatical years in which it was not left fallow, and the purpose of the Israelites' misery in the lands of their enemies is that they may be cured of their stubbornness and thus *atone* for their guilt. When Israel's guilt has been atoned for, YHWH will remember his covenants with Abraham, Isaac, and Jacob; when the land's omitted sabbatical years have been atoned for, YHWH will remember the land.

Surely, all this manipulation—whose purpose is not to deter a vassal from breaking faith, but to encourage a vassal who has broken faith to hope for rehabilitation notwithstanding—takes us well into the sixth century.

It is worth noting that none of the chapters I have dealt with above (Lev 23; Lev 26; Num 28-29) contains any example of those linguistic usages of P which Hurvitz[97] has identified as shibboleths

---

ing that *yimmáqqu* might have which would be a step in the direction of confession, v. 40. Hence "shall be heartsick," as the new JPS Torah translation rightly renders it. For confirmation, see the new JPS Prophets translation (1978) on Ezek 24:15-24, where of course Ezekiel does not tell his fellow exiles—the very remnant destined for survival and restoration (Ezek 11:15-20; 36:16 ff.)—to pine away for their iniquities but to be contrite because of them, 24:22-23.

[97] A Hurvitz, HTR 60 (1967), 117-121; *Tarbiz* 40 (1970-71), 261-67; RB 81 (1974), 24-56.

of relatively early sacerdotal Judean composition. (I prefer this cautious formulation.) Not that the presence of any of them in any other pericope of P necessarily dates it earlier than the seventh century—or even precludes the sixth.[98] After all, the ancestors of those denizens of fifth-century Elephantine who are defined as to territorial origin by the word *yhwdy* (not, very significantly, as **šmry, **d'ry,* or the like), can hardly have migrated to Egypt before ca. 671 B.C.E. (the conquest of the Delta and Memphis by Esarhaddon of Assyria); yet they may have taken the Hebrew word *'eda*[99] with them, since their fifth-century descendants employ in their Aramaic the phrase *qm b'dh w'mr* in connection with the repudiation of a spouse, and it makes no difference for our purpose whether *b'dh* in the Aramaic phrase means in a formal assembly or merely in public. [See Addenda.]

Possibly another example of a characteristic P word which is merely a Judean word that persisted in popular use into the second half of the fifth century B.C.E. is the verb *ma'al.* In P, this verb and the corresponding noun *má'al* are employed mainly in connection with sacrilege, whether this consists in the breach of an oath by YHWH (as in Lev 5:21 ff.) or in the profaning of any of his sancta (Lev 4:15). Ezekiel almost certainly employs the term with technical exactitude in Ezek 15:18, where it presumably refers to Zedekiah's breach of his oath of allegiance to Nebuchadnezzar,[100] and in Ezek 18:24 too he may very well have in mind some offense to which the term *má'al* is properly applicable. He is therefore clearly connected with P, whether one prefers to regard both of them as dependent on a common source or tradition or to make one of them depen-

---

[98] It is a mistake to take the Book of Ezekiel, whose growth and transmission were obviously a complicated process, as a sample of the Hebrew of ca. 600–570, pure and simple. Many of its "late" features surely originated with the prophet's editors and supplementers, and his own Hebrew will hardly have remained unaffected by the vernacular of sixth-century Babylonia. A measure of precision in this as in other matters may be hoped for from the commentary on Ezekiel which is being prepared by Prof. Moshe Greenberg.

[99] Hurvitz, *Tarbiz* 40 (loc. cit.), English summary on pp. 1–11.

[100] Cf. W. Zimmerli, *Ezechiel* (Biblischer Kommentar XIII/1), 1969, p. 318.

dent on the other. Clearly dependent on P are Ezra 9:4 and 10:6.[101]
But the use of the verb *ma'al* in Neh 1:8 and 13:27 is different. In
the former case it occurs in the course of Nehemiah's Deuteron-
omism-studded prayer, Neh 1:5 ff., and in the latter after his
Deuteronomy-styled adjuration, Neh 13:25, of the West Judeans
whose number included men who had married Ashdodite women.
In neither case is it employed in the special sense of sacrilege, but
only with the general meaning of "to break faith with YHWH"—
which makes it strongly reminiscent of Lev 26:40. Since, therefore,
we have seen that Nehemiah gives no evidence of being versed in P,
it would seem that we have here, as in *'eda,* a feature of Judean
speech which persisted in popular usage down into the fifth
century.

---

[101] See above n. 15.

VIII. The Episode of the Golden Calf

This remarkable story is told twice in the Pentateuch: 1. in Exod 24:12–15, 18b; 31:18—34:28; 2. in Deut 9:8—10:8. The first paragraph of the Exod account (24:12–15, 18b) is a flawless piece of E composition: The mountain is—as in the E passages 3:1; 18:5; cf. I Ki 19:5—the Mountain of God (not Mount Sinai), Moses' personal attendant is Joshua, and the deputy leader is Aaron, who, just as in the Amalek episode (17:8–16), has his own junior aide, Hur. However, the purity of the E style has suffered somewhat in the rest of the story, because of the following situation. To begin with, the *E account* of Moses' ascent on the *Mount of God* for the purpose of receiving the *"stone tablets* with the teachings and commandments which I have inscribed to instruct them"* (24:12) is entwined with the *P account* of Moses' ascent on *Mount Sinai,* where he received the *directions for the* construction and furnishing of the *Tabernacle of the Testimony* ('*edut*), 25:21—whose center was to be the *Testimony,* 40:20, deposited in the Ark of the *Testimony,* 40:3,5 (as also directions for the making of the priests' vestments and for the investiture of the priests). And further, either the person who did that entwining or a later one has *partly fused* the two accounts. For he reports the end of both of Moses' sessions with YHWH only with the one statement that "when YHWH finished speaking with Moses on *Mount Sinai* he handed him the two *Tablets* of the *Testimony* (31:32)" and he retains this terminology ever after; e.g. "Mount Sinai," 34:2, 4. One result of this procedure is that one may hesitate between two views of 34:29–35: one may either (a) regard it as the conclusion of the preceding golden calf account or (b) understand it as a link between two parts of the P account, namely, between YHWH's instructions to Moses for the establishment of the Tabernacle etc., in chs. 25–31, on the one hand, and

Moses' report of those instructions to the people in ch. 35, on the other. For we don't really know whether P himself conceived of the Testimony as one stone or two (or as not consisting of stone at all).[102]

Nevertheless, the story of the golden calf in Exodus (apart from the X^D intrusion Exod 34:10–27) must — in view of the important role of Joshua, the less than creditable role which no P writer would have assigned to Aaron,[103] and the fact that (as we shall see) Deuteronomy used it (before its entwining and incipient fusing with P, of course) — be regarded as pre-Deuteronomic and assigned to E. And a very curious tale it is. The forty-day sojourn on the mountain is never really accounted for. In no case was the resulting document so long as to require such a span of time; and if it had been, even a man like the sinewy Moses of Michelangelo could not have carried a weight of stone slabs large enough to be inscribed with such a long text. (And how would they have transported it thereafter?) That the Deuteronomic narrators dwell on the forty days and forty nights at such length in the *second* half of the golden calf story—9:18–19, 25–29 (the JPS Torah Translation of v.25, "*When* I lay prostrate . . . *those* forty days and forty nights . . ." catches the force of the Hebrew idiom); 10:10—shows that they appreciate the fact that the long stay is more appropriate for supplication than for the receiving of a fairly brief text. It is therefore hard to escape the conclusion that the purpose of the pre-golden calf retreat was precisely to provide a plausible background for the people's terrible aberration (Exod 32:1). But then, how and when did the story arise, and why does no extra-

---

[102] It is therefore by no means certain that *'edut* in the passages discussed above means much the same thing as *brit* does in Exod 34:28 and Deut 9:11; and if the above insights had been gained by the mid-1950s, the authors of the JPS Torah translation of 1962 and 1967 might very well have, noncommittally, retained *Testimony* instead of introducing *Pact*.

[103] It may be noted in passing that it was P (or P writers) who not only made Aaron the progenitor of the priestly caste but also made him and his sister Miriam (Exod 15:20; cf. Num 12:1 ff.) siblings of Moses (all three are made children of the same parents in Num 26:59). For the expression in Exod 4:14 means only "your *fellow Levite* Aaron"; so rightly O. Eissfeldt, *Kleine Schriften* IV, Tübingen 1968, pp. 208–9 n., who might have referred to Deut 18:7 for confirmation.

Pentateuchal passage earlier than Ps 106:19-20 and Neh 9:18 know of this black mark against the generation of the wilderness?[104] Clearly, our two golden calf narratives deserve to be scrutinized more closely.

It was explained back in Chapter IV that according to E YHWH and Israel entered at Horeb into a covenant comprising Exod 23:10-33, consisting of ten precepts, embodied in vv.10-19, which Israel undertook to obey, and an obligation, embodied in vv.20-33, which was assumed by YHWH, and that Exod 24:3-8 (an exposition of which is included in our Ch. IV) describes how the covenant was formally solemnized by Moses. (Since we are not told on what sort of material the writing was executed, presumably a soft one—most probably sheepskin—is meant.) When, therefore, we read in Exod 24:12, "YHWH said to Moses, 'Come up to me on the mountain and wait there, and I will give you the stone tablets with the teachings and commandments which I have inscribed to instruct them,'" we are not sure whether it means the covenant which Moses has already reduced to writing in v.4, or something larger including that covenant, or something wholly different. We anticipated in Chs. IV and VI the conclusion that it means only that selfsame covenant of Exod 23:10-33; so that our suspicion that the forty-day sojourn on the mountain (Exod 24:18b) is only introduced in order to supply a plausible explanation for the calf of gold aberration of 32:1 ff. would seem to be confirmed.

Before taking up the latter, however, let us clarify the P strand Exod 24:1-2, 9-10, 16-18a with which the E strand is entwined in Exod 24. The beginning is abrupt, and it is necessary to surmise that a short piece of P text originally connected 19:2a,1,2b with 24:1, containing, perhaps, the information that an angel appeared to the encamped people, or to their leaders, informing them that Mt. Sinai was a very special mountain and that momentous events

---

[104] Ps 106 speaks out of a diaspora (or largely diaspora) situation (Ps 106:47), and it knows Ezekiel's astonishing view that the dispersion was decreed before Israel even entered what was to become its homeland (Ps 106:27, echoing Ezek 20:25).

were due to take place there. Only after some such link as that could the text continue naturally as follows: (24:1) And to Moses he said, "You and Aaron, Nadab and Abihu,[105] and seventy of the elders of Israel, come up closer to YHWH[106] and bow low from a distance; (2) for only Moses shall advance toward YHWH. (As for the people, they shall not even approach with him.)" (9) So Moses and Aaron, Nadab and Abihu, and seventy of the elders of Israel came up closer, (10) and they saw the God of Israel: under his feet was the likeness of a pavement of lapis lazuli, like the very sky for purity. (11) Yet he did not raise his hand against the leaders of the Israelites; they beheld God, and they ate and drank. (16) The Presence of YHWH settled on Mount Sinai. For six days it was hidden by cloud. On the seventh day he called to Moses out of the cloud, (18a) and Moses went inside the cloud and ascended the mountain. (17) Then the Presence of YHWH appeared in the sight of the Israelites as a consuming fire on the top of the mountain.

It is the foregoing, of course, that is continued by the P block 25:1—31:17. The E verses 24:12–15, 18b are only continued by the block 31:18—34:28 (and in 31:18, a fusionist has introduced the P terms *Mount Sinai* and *Testimony*, as we have explained).

Chapter 32 begins logically enough. Moses' prolonged absence has made the people restive. He seems to them to have vanished into thin air. (For even the trait that, when Moses had climbed through the dense cloud that covered the mountain up to where YHWH was, the Presence of YHWH became visible to all the people like a consuming fire at the top of the mountain, 24:16,18a,17, is not an E trait but a P one.) And so they demand of Aaron a "god" to go before them. Aaron feels obliged to comply, but at least takes measures to have the calf regarded as merely a symbol of YHWH, since he builds an altar and proclaims a pilgrimage to the spot for the following day in honor of YHWH.

---

[105] Nadab and Abihu were the two oldest sons of Aaron, Exod 6:23.

[106] Apparently the ground sloped upward toward the foot of the mountain, so that one had to climb an ascent in order to reach it, even if one did not touch the mountain proper.

From here on, however, the story is terribly incoherent.

First, YHWH informs Moses of what is going on and threatens to annihilate the people and make only Moses a great nation. Moses succeeds in getting him to relent by pointing out that the Egyptians are liable to say that taking the Israelites out of Egypt with all that fanfare was merely an act of malice, to lure them into the wilderness and destroy them. Therefore: "(12b) Turn from Your blazing anger, and renounce the plan to bring calamity upon Your people." Surely, another plea after that would be an anti-climax, and logically v.14 should follow here immediately: "(14) And YHWH renounced the calamity he had threatened to bring upon his people." The second argument (v.13), embodying the late idea of YHWH's oath to the Patriarchs,[107] is clearly an afterthought. But actually the whole idea of Moses' being apprised of the people's defection and appeasing YHWH before he even descends from the mountain is secondary.[108] Otherwise, how account for his shocked reaction on witnessing the calf and the crowd dancing before it (v.19)? And why does Moses need to appease YHWH all over again—and with incomplete success (vv.3–14)—if he has already appeased him before coming down from the mountain?

But the incoherence does not end there. According to v.20, Moses' shattering of the tablets is followed immediately by his burning and pulverizing the golden calf. Yet when he rebukes Aaron, Aaron replies as if the calf were still whole: "and out came this calf" (v.24 end). Besides, how could Moses dare to demolish the calf while the people, owing to Aaron's lack of firmness, were so out of control as to be "a menace to any who might oppose

---

[107] See J. Van Seters, VT 22 (1972): 448–59.

[108] YHWH's intimation to Moses of what the people have been up to, and his threat to annihilate them, even before Moses' descent, appears again in Deut 9:12–13; but these verses constitute what Van Seters might call "a blind motif," since Moses there descends without making any attempt to appease YHWH, and he only discovers what has happened when he reaches the camp (Deut 9:16).

them (v.25 end),"[109] so that Moses had to summon his Levite fellow tribesmen to dispose of the mutineers (vv.26–27)? It cannot be denied that logically the place for v.20—"And he took the calf that they had made and, after burning it in fire, beat it fine and strewed it upon the water,[110] thus making the Israelites drink it"—is only after v.29.[111]

Ch. 32 still ends on a harsh note, and it takes our E writer two more chapters to reach the point where YHWH is completely reconciled. E evidently thought it important to tell the story of the golden calf and its terrible consequences in order to induce *his own contemporaries* to give up *their* golden calf, or calves. Perhaps he wrote the story in the early 730's, (i.e. 739–6) when there is reason to believe that Pekah was already ruling Transjordan independently of Menahem, or in 735, when Pekah probably assassinated Menahem's son and successor Pekahiah, or even in 734, when Tiglathpileser of Assyria swept down the East Mediterranean coast

---

[109] In rabbinic literature and Ben Sira, it is true, *šemeṣ/šimṣa* means a suspicion or trace of something (note how in English too "a suspicion" of something can mean a touch or trace of it). But *suspicion* is but a shade removed from *apprehension,* and Tur-Sinai long ago observed (N.H. Tur-Sinai, *The Book of Job,* Jerusalem 1957, pp. 80–81) that only the primary meaning, *fear and trembling,* which is well attested in Arabic, gives sense in Job. Thus in Job 4:12, "my ear took a *šémeṣ* from it," means *"I shuddered to hear it,"* as surely as in Job 29:11, "Any ear that heard declared me blessed, and any eye that saw bore witness on my behalf," means *"Whoever heard* about me declared me blessed, and *whoever saw* me bore witness on my behalf"; and surely Job 26:14ab–b means: *"How frightening* is the sound we hear from him; who can listen to his mighty thunder!" By the same token, in our Exodus passage the above rendering, which is that of the JPS Torah translation, is the only one that does justice to the context.—The Rabbis who sought to account for the disappearance of Hur by surmising that he had been martyred by the ruffians for speaking up (e.g. Bavli Sanh 7a) may have been on the right track.

[110] "The water" means the single source (according to Deut 9:21 it was a brook) from which every person in the camp obtained the water he used, so that everyone would inevitably ingest some water treated with the ashes of the calf; see the following note.

[111] And since the colleagues of R. Yose (Bavli 'Aboda Zara. p. 44a top) were obviously right in maintaining that Moses intended the water mixed with ashes of the golden calf to act, like the water with earth from the floor of the Tabernacle in Num 5:17 ff., as an ordeal producing dire consequences for the guilty, v. 35 (in which in any case *'l 'šr 'bdw* for 'having worshiped' is apparently to be read instead of *'l 'šr 'św* 'for having made') ought to follow immediately on our verse.

to the Egyptian border and—perhaps as a punishment of Pekah for overthrowing the loyal dynasty of Menahem—annexed Israel's coastal plain. Our writer evidently felt that the situation was very critical, and that some warning against the calf fetishism that Second Hosea had inveighed against was necessary.[112]

One Deuteronomist evidently shared E's anxiety, for he incorporated E's golden calf story—complete with the forty days and forty nights—in Deuteronomy. I have pointed out Deuteronomy's borrowings and modifications of elements from E repeatedly, but the strongest proof of Deuteronomy's dependence on E's account of the golden calf episode is that the entire episode is demonstrably secondary in Deuteronomy. In D's original story of Horeb, in Deut 5, there is no abiding on the mountain for forty days; on the contrary, we are told that as soon as YHWH had finished thundering out the Ethical Decalogue (of which the Horeb covenant consisted according to Deut 5:2–5) "he inscribed [it] on two tablets of stone, which he gave to me" (Deut 5:18). It is true that Moses, who was ordered to tell the people who had heard the Ethical Decalogue to return to their tents, stayed on with YHWH in order to receive "the whole Instruction—the laws and the norms—which you shall impart to them, for them to observe in the land that I am giving them to possess" (Deut 5:28). But that cannot have taken forty days and forty nights, for when Moses does impart it to them—just under forty years later—it turns out to have comprised rather less than our present Book of Deuteronomy. Yet in 9:8–9 he recalls: "(8) Thus at Horeb you so provoked YHWH that YHWH was angry enough with you to have destroyed you. (9) It was when I ascended the mountain to receive the tablets of stone, the Tablets of the Covenant that YHWH had made with you, and stayed on the mountain forty days and forty nights eating no bread and drinking no water." There follows the story of the giving of the Tablets,

---

[112] Exod 32:34b may even be intended to hint that Israel's *current woes* were decreed, for this very sin, back in the wilderness period, which would make this half-verse a forerunner of Ezek 20:23.

Moses' descent from the mountain, and the horrible thing he discovered when he came to the camp. But this comes as a complete
surprise after ch. 5. For there (Deut 5:2–17), after repeating the
Ethical Decalogue as the covenant that YHWH had made with
Israel at Horeb — that was thundered out by YHWH from the
midst of the fire and the black cloud — Moses adds (v.18[19]):
"YHWH spoke those words—those and no more—to your whole
congregation at the mountain . . ., and he inscribed them on two
tablets of stone, which he gave to me." The episode of Moses'
forty-day-long absence, the mischief the people got into as a
result, and the ensuing complications and their resolution, is an
afterthought inspired by E's account in Exodus, and it shows it by
other features which we have already pointed out. It reflects
Israelian conditions, for both E and D are Israelian documents,
and it bulks large in "The Israelian Heritage of Judaism."

IX. Deuteronomy and the Book of Isaiah

At the beginning of Section II, I wrote: "It can be shown that Deuteronomy is strongly influenced by the diction of the Israelian Book of Hosea (both in primary and in secondary passages), that it also adopts Hosean ideas, and that it even legislates measures in response to Hosean denunciations, whereas it borrows from Isaiah only diction and literary devices, and those only in secondary passages; and that, conversely, only post-Isaian passages in the Book of Isaiah are indebted to Deuteronomy. If this is demonstrated, it will follow that Proto-Deuteronomy arose in a different area from Isaiah and before Isaiah had become a classic, in other words, in the kingdom of Israel between about 740 and 725 B.C.E." The various influences received by Deuteronomy from the Book of Hosea (and from other Israelian sources) have already been amply illustrated. To complete the picture, we shall add here a few examples of borrowings from Isaiah in secondary passages of Deuteronomy and borrowings from Deuteronomy in secondary passages of Isa 1–33. (It is not necessary to cite examples from Isa 34–66, since it is well known that no part of this block was authored by Isaiah himself except, perhaps, 37:22b–29 [33–35?].)

1. Reflexes of Isaiah in Deuteronomy

(a) The phrase *naśa țórah* 'to bear a burden,' Deut 1:12, is no doubt borrowed from Isa 1:14, since not only the phrase but the unusual noun *țórah* is limited to these two passages. (The common word for 'burden' *maśśa* also occurs in combination with the verb *naśa,* Jer 17:21,27.) The echo from Isa 1:14 occurs in the course of the *later* introduction to Deuteronomy, 1:1—4:43. (The earlier one begins at Deut 4:44.)

(b) The inspiration for the uncannily swift and voracious nation "from afar, from the end of the earth," Deut 28:43–51, is obviously Isa 5:26–29 (for *wš'g* in v.29, which is contaminated by the opening word in that verse, rd. *wšnym* 'and teeth,' cf. Ps 58:7). Note that the entire Deuteronomic phrase *goy merahoq miqqse ha'ares* agrees almost syllable for syllable with the Isaian *goy mimmerhaq . . . miqqse ha'ares*, in which *goy mimmerhaq*—cf. Jer 5:15—is read, with others, for MT's *goyim merahoq* in view of the singulars 'to it' and 'it shall come' in this verse and all the singulars in the following ones. Is, then, Deut 28:49–51 part of a secondary passage in Deuteronomy? I have already remarked, in passing, that the curses of Deut 28 at one time no doubt practically concluded with vv.45–46, since their immediate continuation is—inevitably—anticlimactic,[113] (though v.68 could have followed v.48 directly).

(c) Deut 31:1—32:47 is notoriously not even a continuation of the later conclusion to D (which is usually agreed to be chs. 29–30, probably beginning with 28:69 of the printed Hebrew Bibles) but rather a still later supplement. It is therefore not surprising to find that the notion of putting a text down in writing to serve as a witness against a future generation, Deut 31:19–21, is borrowed from Isa 30:8, where of course the ancient versions enumerated in *Biblia Hebraica Stuttgartensia* ad loc. are to be followed in interpreting the consonants *l'd* as *l'ed* 'for a witness.' Now, the very text which, according to Deut 31:19–21, Moses is to inscribe for a witness, namely the Song of Moses, Deut 32:1–43, is itself largely inspired by Isaiah. For the leading motif of the Song, namely that the Israelites are faithless children of YHWH, 32:5–6, 15–19, is a well-known Isaian one; see not only the verse that follows the one (Isa 30:8) that has already been referred to but also Isa 1:2–4, and moreover the opening half-verse 2a is remarkably suggestive of Deut 32:1,3. In fact, the phrase *banim mašhitim* 'depraved children' of Isa 1:4 is probably to be restored in the obviously corrupt half-

---

[113] See above, p. 20 n. 20 end.

verse Deut 32:5a. Here, first of all, *šht* is to be placed between the first and last *m*'s of *mwmm* and then the last two words are to be placed first, yielding *bnyw mw mšḥtm lw l'*; and this last, in turn, is to be corrected to *bnym mšḥtm yld* "He has begotten depraved children." For the resulting *banim*, 5a//*dor*, 5b, cf. *dor*, 20ba//*banim*, 20bb.[113a]

The Song of Moses reflects a colossal national calamity and an intense longing for vengeance and for a return of YHWH's favor. At the time of the collapse of the kingdom of Israel in 722, Isaiah cannot yet have attained there such a dissemination and prestige as are reflected in Deut 31–32, and besides the Song also exhibits points of contact with Jeremiah, which again are no doubt due to borrowing on the part of the Song.[114] Add to this the parallelism in content between the Song and Isa 63:7—64:11 to which Fohrer calls attention,[115] and there is really no escaping the conclusion that the background of the Song is the woeful situation after the destruction of the kingdom of Judah in 586 B.C.E.

2. Echoes of Deuteronomy in Isa 1–33

(a) In Isa 4:3, the phrase *hnš'r bṣywn whnwtr byrwšlm* is inspired by a phrase in Deut 7:20, namely, *hnš'rym whnwtrym* (so read for the inapposite *whnstrym* of MT). One reason for regarding Isa 4:3 as post-Isaian has already been given in passing: the peculiar practice of regarding all the members of a temple community as domiciled in the temple city though many are not so in fact.[116] Our verse is continued by vv.4 ff., of which v.4 contains the telltale verb *hediaḥ*

[113a] The dependent character of the Song is confirmed by the reversal in v. 1 of the normal order of the parallel synonyms *šama'*//*he'ĕzin*. See below n. 136.

[114] (a) Jer 2:27b–28a/Deut 32:35bb, 37–38. In v. 35bb, emendation of *'tdt* to *'t r'h* is required by its parallelism to *ywm 'yd* in v. ba and by *lywm* (so rightly Samaritan and Septuagint)//*l't* in the a-verse, cf. *Tarbiz* 24 (1954-55), p. 2 *Perush*, para. 4; (b) Jer 8:18/Deut 32:21ab.

[115] G. Fohrer, *Introduction to the Old Testament*, English translation Nashville-New York 1968, p. 190. See also G. von Rad on this chapter in his commentary on *Deuteronomy*, English translation, Westminster Press, Philadelphia, 1966.

[116] See n. 6a.

'to rinse or flush,' which only appears in place of *šaṭap* from Ezek 40:38 and II Chron 4:6 on. (In Jer 51:34, where the received reading is inapposite, *hĕriqáni* 'he emptied me out,' is probably to be read.) As for Isa 4:5–6, if the first word in v.5 is emended to *uparaś* it will be seen that "YHWH will spread . . . cloud . . . and . . . canopy (*wsukka,* v.6)" is borrowed from Ps 105:39. (This has *masak,* a different word from our *sukka,* but one derived from the same root *skk* and meaning the same thing—the idea of the cloud serving not to lead but to shade goes back, in turn, to Num 10:34.)—The extreme lateness of Ps 105 is apparent enough from such features as (i) *mašíah* meaning simply (God's) 'chosen one' without reference to any anointment (v.15), a usage which is first attested by Deutero-Isaiah (Isa 45:1; cf. the finite verb *mašah* meaning simply 'to single out' [said of God] in Isa 61:1); (ii) *lo hinníah* (v.14) 'he did not let (somebody do something)' instead of the classical *lo natan* (as e.g. in Gen 20:6, in the very passage, Gen 20:3–7, on which our author obviously drew for the notions of God rebuking a king on account of a Patriarch and of a Patriarch being also a prophet), the only other biblical occurrences of *lo hinníah* being those in I Chron 16:21; Koh 5:11; (iii) *'amal* 'gains, wealth' (v.44)—postbiblical but also frequent in Koheleth; (iv) such late elements of tradition as the covenant with the Patriarchs (vv.8–11,42)[117] and the Joseph story (vv.17–22). [See Addenda.]

(b) Isa 30:22 is clearly influenced by Deut 7:25–26. The latter admonishes Israel, before it invades Canaan, with reference to *the idols of the indigenous population:* "(Deut 7:25) . . . you shall not covet any silver or gold on them and keep it for yourself . . . (26) You must not bring an abhorrent thing into your house . . .; you must detest and abhor it. . . ." Isa 30:22, for its part, predicts that Israel, in its eschatological repentance, will adopt exactly that attitude toward *its own idols:* "(Isa 30:22a) Then you will treat as unclean (an estimative, not factitive, piel) the silver overlay of your images and the golden plating of your idols." We are even able to explain why

---

[117] See above n. 107.

our author says "treat as unclean" instead of Deuteronomy's "detest and abhor" thanks to the next half-verse, which at the same time shows that our man knew P as well as D: "(Isa 30:22b) You will keep them away (vocalize *tazzirem*, cf. Lev 15:31) like a menstruous woman (cf. Lev 15:33). 'Out!' you will call to them." For the passage Lev 15:31-33, which our author clearly had in mind, employs five times the root *ṭm'* 'to be unclean.'

(c) The next two verses in Isa 30 (vv.23-24) which describe the prosperity with which Israel's conversion will be rewarded, are clearly an elaboration of Deut 11:14-15: Israel will not only have abundant rain to produce its food crops but the resulting food will be rich and fat. And Israel's livestock will have not only the herbage it needs but (i) its nonworking livestock will have wide pastures to graze, and (ii) its beasts of farm labor will live in positive luxury, partaking of "salted(?) fodder that has been winnowed with shovel and fan."

No wonder, then, that Isa 30:19 again illustrates the late practice of speaking as if the entire population of Judah resided in Zion,[118] while v.26 employs for 'moon' and 'sun' the well-known post-biblical terms *lbana* and *ḥamma* whose only other biblical occurrences are in Isa 24:23 (from ca. 400 B.C.E.[119]) and in Solomon's Song 6:10 (hardly pre-third century).

To repeat, the author of Proto-Deuteronomy (though profoundly influenced by the Israelian Book of Hosea because he is a fellow countryman of the two Hoseas and is close in time to Second Hosea) is uninfluenced by Isaiah because he is a contemporary of the still young Isaiah and resides in a different kingdom from him. And for the same reason the genuine Isaiah is uninfluenced by Deuteronomy.

---

[118] See above n. 6a.

[119] See *The Book of Isaiah A New Translation,* Introduction by H. L. Ginsberg, Jewish Publication Society of America, 1973, Introduction p. 14 [12], para. 2.

X. Direct Influences of the Book of Hosea
on Seventh-Century Judah and Its Successors

We have seen how profoundly the Book of Hosea influenced Deuteronomy, and through Deuteronomy all subsequent Yahwism. But it would be a mistake to suppose that the Book of Hosea did not, in addition, affect the Judites directly. Thus, it may cheerfully be granted that in Isa 63:8b–9aa the Septuagint reading[120] is the correct one, and that its immediate parent is not the polemic against trust in angels in Hos 12[121] but Deut 4:37b.[122] But the same Second Isaiah constructs his sermon on vain fasting, Isa 58:1–5, on the model of Hos 8:1–2; 7:14,[123] and owes his thrice recorded prediction that even those parts of Israel's land which always were desert will become verdant (Isa 35:1–2; 51:3acd; 65:10) to Hos 2:16–17 [14–15].[124]

But the prophet whose borrowings from the Book of Hosea include at least one fateful one, is Jeremiah. To appreciate its importance, however, one must appreciate the difference between First and Second Hosea. I have clarified my views on this problem—building on the work of Graetz and Y. Kaufmann—in my article "Hosea" in *Encyclopaedia Judaica*,[125] to which the reader is

---

[120] It yields the sense: "So he was their deliverer (9) in all their troubles. No angel or messenger, his own person delivered them." That this was the sense intended is confirmed by the next sentence: ". . . he himself redeemed them."

[121] See above, p. 20.

[122] "In his great might, he in person freed you from Egypt."—Similarly, Isa 52:12aa presupposes Deut 16:3ba.

[123] As I pointed out in *Hebräische Wortforschung—Festschrift Walter Baumgartner* (VTS 16), 1967, p. 76 top.

[124] See the section headed "Recovering the Original Text of Hos 2: 16–17" in *Yehezkel Kaufmann Jubilee Volume* 1960, pp. 67–69.

[125] See *Encyclopaedia Judaica* 8, cols. 1010 ff.

referred. Here I repeat only this much: Hosea A (chs.1–3) embodies the message of Hosea son of Beeri, who prophesied shortly
after the introduction of the Baal cult by Ahab (say between 870
and 865 B.C.E.), when it was essentially limited to a small court cir-
cle. That is why he introduces the allegorical figure of YHWH's
guilty "wife" (official Israel) alongside the personally innocent children, whom he calls upon to rebuke their mother (2:4[2]) in their
own interest. Hosea himself is included in this command to
rebuke, for although he is certainly not personally guilty he is
included in "you are not my people" (1:9; the *you* is plural, Heb
'attem), because of guilt "by association." Only this unique situation accounts for the appearance of the wife allegory at this junc-
ture, and after that it vanishes for two hundred and fifty years.[126]
Jeremiah, however, who borrows from Hosea B (Hos chs. 4–14,
745–40 B.C.E.) the view that YHWH was delighted with Israel in the
wilderness and that it only went astray on coming to settled country (Hos 9:10; Jer 2:2—3,7–8), also borrows from Hosea A the wife
metaphor (beginning Jer 2:2). Why? Because, speaking during
"the second period of official paganism," after the long reign of
Manasseh (plus Amon) and before the eighteenth year of Josiah, he
is struck by the aptness of the comparison of this apostasy to adul-
tery. However, "Manassism" had lasted so long (probably seven
decades) that Jeremiah was unable to take over from Hosea the
distinction between an erring mother and children who were guilty
only through collective responsibility. Jeremiah (2:8,26–29; 3:21;
5:1,9,23,26,31; 6:27–30; 8:6–7; 9:1–8; 25:1 ff.; 35:15) speaks of
the nation generally as idolatrous and corrupt. That is why when
he revives Hosea's wife allegory he also simplifies it, omitting the
children. (Jer 3:14–17 is not a continuation of vv. 11–13 but a
separate utterance.)[127]

But there is more. If Hos 2:1–3[1:10—2:1] is transferred to the

---

[126] Against the interpretation of any passages in Hosea B as embodying this allegory, see
Encylcopaedia Judaica, ibid., cols. 1010 bottom–1019 top.
[127] Ibid. col. 1016.

end of ch.2, as is done by many, and if the likewise non-figurative 2:20[18] is moved down to follow that block, then the announcement of the termination of the literal God-people covenant between YHWH and Israel (1:9) is followed immediately by a translation into the language of allegory: YHWH's wife is no longer his wife and he is no longer her husband. The allegory is continued without interruption until, in 2:21–22[19–20], we have the promise of a new espousal with a built-in guarantee that it will never be annulled; for YHWH will bestow upon the bride as brideprice (since she has no father to whom it can be paid)—for the *b-* in *'eraś b-* is the *b-* of price (witness II Sam 3:14b)—certain qualities which will make her constitutionally incapable of disloyalty. The literal equivalent of that is obviously the making with Israel of a new covenant with a built-in guarantee against Israel's breaking it, in the shape of a change in Israel that will make loyalty to YHWH not a habit that is learned, or second nature, but instinct, or "first nature." And in this case Jeremiah, with his "new covenant," has, instead of adopting Hosea's wife metaphor, supplied its nonfigurative explication, Jer 31:30–33[31–34] (cf.32:39–40).

Jeremiah's emulators, Ezekiel and Second Isaiah, have adopted, in addition to varieties of his new covenant (Ezek 36:24–29a; Isa 54:14), the wife allegory, to which they restore the children alongside the wife (Ezek 16:20; Isa 49:17–21). How this revived allegory eventually led to the allegorical interpretation of the Song of Solomon, has been shown by G.D. Cohen.[128]

[128] G.D. Cohen, 'The Song of Songs and the Jewish Religious Mentality,' *The Samuel Friedland Lectures,* 1960–66, New York 1966, pp. 1–21.

POSTSCRIPT

In pointing out (in Chapter VII) that Lev 23:22 is an adaptation of Lev 19:9–10, I have implied that there are parts of H (=Lev 17–26[27]), or the Holiness Code, that are older than the late (post-D and post-X^D) catalogue of special days Lev 23. Such a relatively early section is "The Mount Sinai Covenant" (Lev 25–26, note particularly 26:9, 11–12)—minus, of course, the patently post-catastrophe block 26:39–45, with which vv. 34–35 are probably connected (see Chapter VII, d). For Sara Japhet has shown that an entire pericope in Deuteronomy, namely Deut 15, is adapted from Exod 21:2–11 plus Lev 25.[129] At the same time, in view of the numbered-month reflex of the Assyro-Babylonian calendar in Lev 25:9, even the basic stock of H can hardly date from before the seventh century B.C.E. (see above, Chapter VII).

Whereas, however, the influence of H on Deut 15 presumably dates from before the Babylonian exile, reflexes in Deuteronomy of the Priestly Code (P) apart from the H elements would seem to date from postexilic times and to be confined mainly to references to the divine promises made to all three of the Patriarchs, Abraham, Isaac, and Jacob. For here I must take issue with those portions of two partly overlapping papers by J. Milgrom which claim that certain ideas of Deuteronomy are derived from the Priestly Code.[130] Milgrom believes that the concept of the God-

---

[129] S. Japhet in Studies in Bible and the Ancient Near East Presented to Samuel E. Loewenstamm on His Seventieth Birthday, Jerusalem 1978, Hebrew Volume pp. 231–249; English abstract, titled 'The laws of manumission of slaves and the question of the relationship between the laws in the Pentateuch,' in English Volume pp. 199–200.

[130] J. Milgrom, 'Profane slaughter and a formulaic key to the composition of Deuteronomy,' HUCA 47 (1976), pp. 1–17; Idem, 'A formulaic key to the composition of Deuteronomy,' Eretz Israel 14 (1978), Hebrew section pp. 42–47. (English summary in English section pp. 123 f.) Both in the HUCA paper, p. 10 n. 33, and in Eretz Israel 114, p. 45 n. 23,

people relationship between YHWH and Israel originated with P, and that making it a two-way covenant was an innovation of D (Deut 26:17–18). However, both the idea of the God-people relationship and the belief that it was based on a two-way covenant are far older than P, or even D.

Deut 32:1–43 was composed later than Jeremiah (see above, Chapter IX, 1 [c]). Yet it dates YHWH's adoption of Israel as his people during the desert wanderings that preceded its establishment in its historical homeland, Deut 32:9–14.[131] In this regard it agrees with the earlier sources.

Another very early testimony concerning the tradition of the establishment of the God-people relationship is that of Hosea son

---

the author acknowledges indebtedness to Y. Muffs, 'Covenantal traditions in Deuteronomy,'—lectures at The Jewish Theological Seminary, 1965.

[131] One should not be misled by some apparent archaisms in grammar and vocabulary. Thus the pronominal suffix -énhu for standard -énnu (Deut 32:10c,d) occurs again only in the Song by the Sea, namely in Exod 15:2 (where to the preserved form 'arommenhu 'odénhu, to which the ghost word 'anwéhu must be corrected in light of Isa 25:1; Ps 118:28). Very archaic is the diction. Note first of all v. 6b: 'abíka-qqanéka . . . waykonnéka, with which cf. both Ugaritic abh//dyknnh (CTA no. 4,/IV 47–48) 'his father//who begot him' and kqnyn (l[m]//kdrd<r>dyknn [   ] (CTA no. 10, III, 6–7); for clearly, both in Deut 32:6b and in the last cited Ugaritic passage the context suggests for the root qny the sense of 'to engender' (as in the prose verse Gen 4:1). Similarly, dam 'enab, Deut 32:14, 'blood of grapes' (i.e. wine) recalls not only yáyin//dam 'anabim 'wine//blood of grapes,' Gen 49:11 (in an old blessing of the tribe of Judah) but also Ugaritic yn//dm 'ṣm (in which the second term presumably means 'blood of grapevines'). Finally, the word par'ot in our v. 42 is the construct state of pra'ot, Jud 5:2, whose antiquity is universally recognized. Occurring only in these two pasages, the noun designates fighting men and would seem to mean literally 'longhairs' (cf. péra' 'untrimmed [hair],' Num 6:4; Ezek 44:20) because of a presumable custom of leaving the hair of the head unshorn for the duration of a military campaign. In any case, it was probably because he associated pr'wt with the said péra' that somebody was led to substitute—deliberately or inadvertently—mr's 'from the heads of' for what I believe was an original ms'r, i.e. miss'er 'from the bodies of,' in Deut 32:42. For the ancient Israelite's sword was notoriously so short (the length of Ehud's sword is given as one cubit, Jud 3:15) that when attached to his belt it was said to rest "on his thigh" (Jud 3:14, 21; Song of Solomon 3:6). To strike an intended victim in the head with it would therefore have been impractical; contrast the efficient slayings in Jud 3:21; II Sam 3:27; 4:6; 20:10.

The following annotated translation of Deut 32:40–42 will probably be found useful:
40 For I will lift my hand to the sky
    and will swear,
"As I live forever!

of Beeri. The message of this prophet, whom we also style "First
Hosea," dates from the second quarter of the ninth century B.C.E.
and is contained in Hos chs. 1–3 (see above, Chapter X). In Hos
1:9, the seer is informed by YHWH that because of Israel's breach
of faith, "You (*'attem,* plural, meaning Hosea and his fellow
countrymen) are not my people, and I am not your God"; but in
Hos 2:25[23] YHWH promises that in a happier future "I will say
to Not-My-People 'You are my people,' and he will respond, 'You
are my God.'" Obviously, Hosea envisages the reestablishment of
the God-people relationship as a two-way pact, which alone
would suggest that he also conceived of the original establishment
of the relationship as a two-way covenant. Fortunately, there is
direct confirmation for this surmise, as we know now thanks to an
exegetical insight of M.A. Friedman.[132] Briefly, it is this. In the
husband-wife allegory of Hos 2:4–25[2–23], the sentence (v.
17b[15b]) "She will respond . . . as in the days of her youth, at the
time when she came up from the land of Egypt" means "She will
respond to my wooing (v. 16[14]) with 'You are my husband' just as
she did the first time." (With the difference, to be sure, that this
time she will be careful to employ for 'husband' the Hebrew word

---

41 When I whet my flashing blade
    and my hand grasps my bow,*
    I'll wreak vengeance on my foes,
    retribution** on my enemies.
42a I'll make my arrows drunk with blood
  c from the blood of battle-slain and captives,
  b and my sword shall devour flesh
  d from the bodies*** of enemy longhairs.

   *Reading *bqaŝti* in view of 42a. So already *Tarbiz* 24 (1954/5), p. 2 n. 12a.
   **Probably read *ŝillem* as in v. 38.
   ***Read *miŝŝ'er*; so already *Tarbiz* ibid. p. 3 n. 14.

But obviously all such *a priori* considerations are outweighed by the evidence of dependence on Isaiah, Jeremiah, and Lamentations, just as historico-critical philology is right in
maintaining the sixth-century dating of Deutero-Isaiah in spite of such "Ugariticisms" as *yr'*
// *ŝt' (ŝt' // yr')* and *ks* // *qb't.*
[132] M.A. Friedman, JBL 99 (1980), pp. 199–204.

'*iš* and will—for a reason that is obvious from vv. 10[8] and
15[13]—avoid its synonym *bá'al*, vv. 18–19[16–17].)[133] In non-
allegorical language, of course, that means that, in the new covenant as in the old, Israel will respond to YHWH's 'You are my
people' with 'You are my God'; cf. the already cited v. 25[23]. The
idea of the God-people relationship between YHWH and Israel
did not, therefore, originate in Gen 17:7 or Exod 6:7. Indeed,
both these verses have a tag marked "exilic or postexilic" attached
to them. For Gen 17:7 is followed by Gen 17:8, which embodies
the exilic notion of YHWH's unconditional promise to Abraham
to bestow the land of Abraham's sojourning as a gift in perpetuity
upon his descendants, while the pericope Exod 6:1–8 is perhaps
the most striking single proof of the postexilic date of P, since it
embodies the same promise—expressed in v. 4 by the term "I
established my covenant" and in v. 8 by "I swore"—with all three
of the Patriarchs (Abraham, Isaac, and Jacob) as the recipients.[134]
These passages cannot be preexilic because in the preexilic tradition the God-people relationship was established with, and possession of the land was promised to, the generation of the Exodus.

That First Hosea speaks, in allegorical terms, of the first covenant as having been entered into "at the time when she came up
from the land of Egypt," we have already seen. Over a century
later, another Israelian prophet, Second Hosea (the prophet of
Hos 4–14) sings of how delighted YHWH was with Israel during
the desert wandering that preceded its arrival at Baal-peor (Hos
9:10) and of how YHWH "fell in love with Israel when it was a
child and called it 'my son' from the land of Egypt on" (11:1); and

---

[133] Thus the repointing I proposed for *w'nth* (Hos 2:17)[15] in *Yehezkel Kaufmann Jubilee
Volume,* Jerusalem 1960 English section p. 69, becomes superfluous. However, the other
emendations proposed for the passage in question on pp. 67–69 ibid. are still necessary.

[134] See J. Van Seters, 'Confessional reformulation in the exilic period,' VT 22 (1972), pp.
449–459. In this article, the Pentateuch passages which Van Seters proves to be exilic by the
criterion in question all belong to the traditional JE corpus; but he applies it *a fortiori* to the
postexilic source P in the course of his volume *Abraham in History and Tradition.* New Haven
and London 1975, in which see, for example, pp. 289, 311, 313.

he has YHWH declare twice, "I YHWH have been your God ever since the land of Egypt" (12:10[9]; 13:4). Again, when Amos (the Judite who prophesied to Israelian audiences) delivers *"to . . . the family that I brought up from the land of Egypt"* a message from YHWH which begins with the statement (Amos 3:2) "You alone have I singled out from all the families of the earth," does he not imply that the singling out took place in the generation of the Exodus?

It was no different with Judite prophets addressing Judite audiences. Thus Jer 7:22 f. reads as follows: "(22) For *when I took your fathers out of the land of Egypt . . . (23) this is how I charged them:* Do my bidding, and *I will be your God and you will be my people . . ."* Further, Jeremiah predicts (Jer 31:31–34 [32–33]) that YHWH will make with the House of Israel and the House of Judah a new *covenant* which shall differ from the one *he made with them at the time when he freed them from Egypt* in that this time YHWH will take measures to make those two "Houses" constitutionally incapable of breaking it, so that he will not, in turn, renounce it. In this way, *"I will be their God and they shall be my people"* (scil. forever, see Jer 32:38–40).[135]

---

[135] However, if the Song of Moses and Second Hosea could speak of the election of Israel without reference to oaths or covenants, it is not surprising to find that Jeremiah does the same in Jer 31:1–5[30:25—31:4], in which he bases his hope for the rehabilitation of Ephraim on the love which, echoing Hos 9:10, he declares that YHWH conceived for Israel in the wilderness (it is also implied by Deut 32:10–12); he merely adds that the love YHWH conceived for Israel on that occasion was an undying love and is still alive. Here is a translation of the pasage, for which cf. NJPS: "(Jer 31:1) At that time—declares YHWH—I will be God to all the clans of Israel, and they shall be my people. (2) Thus said YHWH: The people escaped from the sword found favor in the wilderness; when Israel was marching homeward, (3) YHWH revealed himself to it of old. Eternal love I conceived for you then; therefore I continue my grace to you. (4) I will build you firmly again, O Maiden Israel! Again you shall take up your timbrels and go forth to the rhythm of the dancers. (5) Again you shall plant vineyards on the hills of Samaria; men shall plant and live to enjoy them." The words were spoken prior to the collapse of Judah (cf. v. 6[5]); but further on we shall see Second Isaiah, who is late exilic and therefore knows the late exilic Abraham ideology, similarly dispense with any mention of YHWH swearing to or covenanting with Abraham but merely stress, in highly lyrical terms, such an outpouring of divine grace upon the Patriarch that the Jacob-Israel of the prophet's own day may face the future with buoyant anticipation.

Ezekiel, a priest who was among the captives deported by Nebuchadnezzar on the surrender of King Joiachin in the year 597 (II Ki 24:12–16), and was convinced that the remaining population of Judah would likewise be exiled to Babylonia, began to prophesy to his fellow exiles in 593. In the year 591 (Ezek 20:1) he produced a characteristically dour survey of the history of the God-people relationship from its inception to date and an equally harsh, even though favorable, prediction of the future (Ezek ch. 20). Needless to say, he dates the inception of the relationship, which he explicitly makes the occasion for the promise of the land as well, in the generation of the Exodus, though not after but before the departure from Egypt (Ezek 20:5–6). To quote: "(5) In the day that I chose Israel, I gave my oath to the stock of Jacob; when I made myself known to them in the land of Egypt, I swore this oath to them, 'I YHWH am your God.' (6) On that day I swore to them to take them out of the land of Egypt to a land flowing with milk and honey, a land which I had sought out for them, the one which is the desire of all the nations" (lit. "lands," but cf. Ezekiel's source Jer 3:19).

To be sure, Ezekiel goes on to say that YHWH made his promise conditional on the Israelites' absolute loyalty. Yet, though they clung to "the detestable things they were drawn to, and held fast to the fetishes of Egypt," YHWH was deterred from annihilating them then and there by concern for his holy name, which would be profaned in the sight of the surrounding "nations" (pl!), since he had entered into his relationship with Israel in their sight. After that, twice in the wilderness YHWH would have annihilated the Israelites but for the same deterrent; and even now, after—for good and sufficient reasons—exiling them from their land, he will restore them to it, only from the same motive (Ezek 20:41–44; cf. 36:16–32).

And as we saw in Chapter VII, paragraph d, this ground for hope is adopted—no doubt from Ezekiel—by the first post-catastrophe supplementer of Lev 26 (in Lev 26:44–45).

Now, we also read in Exod 32 that when YHWH revealed to
Moses his wish, because of the golden calf aberration, to annihilate
the Israelites (with the exception of Moses, whom he would make
the ancestor of a great nation) Moses pleaded (Exod 32:12), "The
Egyptians may think, 'It was with malice (aforethought) that he
took them out, only to slay them in the hills and wipe them off the
face of the earth.'" But this plea does not strike us as odd because
the scene of the golden calf incident was Horeb, and it therefore
took place only, at most, a few months after the Exodus (cf. P's
date of the arrival at Sinai, Exod 19:1). Conceivably, therefore, the
Egyptians might hear of the holocaust perpetrated by YHWH
upon the erstwhile slave population that he had wrenched from
their grasp. And when Moses makes a similar plea in Num
14:13–16, against YHWH's carrying out his threat to annihilate the
Israelites for their loss of nerve as a result of the report brought
back by the scouts about the formidable strength and even terrify-
ing stature of the inhabitants of the Holy Land, we do not find that
odd either, since the scouting expedition took place within a year
of the Exodus. But as for Ezekiel and his emulator in Lev 26:44–45,
one may well wonder whether, supposing that there had already
been available at the beginning of the Babylonian exile a doctrine
of YHWH's unconditional promise to Abraham to bestow the land
in perpetuity upon his descendants, those writers would have had
recourse to such a "metaphysical" doctrine as that of YHWH's
having entered into his God-people relationship with the Israelites
"in the sight of the nations," who — still remembering it now,
something like six centuries later — must needs regard Israel's
exile as hopelessly damaging to YHWH's reputation unless he
redeems it by restoring Israel's fortunes. For as we have seen
(again in Chapter VII), the latest supplementer of Lev 26 was glad
to cite the doctrine, which had meanwhile evolved, of the covenants with the Patriarchs (Lev 26:42).

Before explaining the genesis of this new doctrine, let us first
complete the evidence that in the preexilic view the (conditional)
promise of the land, like the establishment of the God-people

relationship, dates from the generation of the Exodus. In addition to the testimonies of the preexilic prophets, the early exilic prophet Ezekiel, and Ezekiel's emulator in Lev 26:44–45, we have those of two preexilic narratives in the Pentateuch. Thus the Mount Sinai Covenant of Lev 25–26, which is named in the opening paragraph of this Postscript, promises that, as a reward for Israel's obedience, "(26:9b) I will establish my covenant with you . . . (11b) and I will not spurn you. (12) I will be ever present in your midst; I will be your God, and you shall be my people. (13) I YHWH am your God, who brought you out of the land of the Egyptians to be their slaves no more, who broke the bars of your yoke and made you walk erect." There is of course not a word here about YHWH's having already been "the God of your fathers" and about his having already established a covenant with them.[136] Also, though it

---

[136] To be sure, v. 42 does give as a reason why YHWH will relent (when Israel has atoned for its guilt) YHWH's covenants with Jacob, Isaac, and Abraham. But I have already classified that verse among the latest post-catastrophe expansions of Lev 26, and here is an interesting additional reason: A genuine P passage which names the covenants with all three of the Patriarchs is Exod 6:2–9, which actually mentions the promise to all three of the Patriarchs twice, once in vv. 2–3 as a covenant and once in v. 8 as an oath, and both times in their natural—chronological—order. The remarkable anachronistic order in which Lev 26:42 lists them is (combined with *the scriptio plena* of the Hebrew form of "Jacob," which is rare even in late passages) a sign of borrowing. So is the analogous reversal which I mention in the latter part of Chapter VII: The First Hosea-Deuteronomy triad new grain-new wine-new oil, which those two sources always list in that order because it is the one in which nature ripens the crops involved, is borrowed in the opposite, counter-calendaric, order in the P verse Num 18:12. Analogous is the tendency, discussed by Moshe Zaidl (משה זיידל), Sinai 38 (5716 A.M.–1956 C.E.), pp. 148 , for later biblical versifiers to reverse some *a* and *b* synonyms of their models. Although some of his alleged examples are unusable because his datings of the sources involved is precritical, there is one which becomes very impressive just when the critical dating of one of the sources involved is adopted. Where, namely, Second Hosea employs 'to fornicate' as a word and *niṭma* 'to defile oneself' as *b*-word (Hos 5:3b and 6:10b), Ps 106 (on whose late date see above Chapter VIII) not only inverts the two roots but strains the meaning of one of them as follows, Ps 106:39: Thus they became unclean (*wayyiṭm'u*) by their deeds and "dissolute" (*wayyiznu*) by their practices. ("Their" in both cases refers to the Canaanites, *to whose gods* the Israelites *sacrificed* their children.) The same principle strikingly confirms that the parallel passages in the Song of Moses and the words of Isaiah are indeed due to borrowing by the former from the latter and not *vice versa*. For the order of the parallel synonyms *šama'* and *he'ĕzin* in Isa 1:2 is the same as not only in Isa 1:10 and 32:9 but also in Gen 4:21; Num 23:18, Micah 6:2 (where with others, correct *wh'ytnym* to *wh'zynw*). Therefore, the testimony of the reverse order in

promises the land explicitly in 25:38 and again implicitly in 26:5-6, it does, not represent the covenant as a two-way agreement. But there is another, considerably older, Pentateuch version, which was the subject of Chapter IV section 2, above, where it was assigned to the E (= Ephraimite) source. Its terms, it may be recalled, are those ten precepts that are enjoined upon Israel in Exod 23:10-19 on the one hand, and YHWH's promises which are embodied in vv. 20 ff., on the other. In these verses YHWH promises, first, to bring Israel to "the place which I have made ready (v. 20)"—with of course never a hint that it has already been promised to the Patriarchs as a possession for their descendants— and, then, to enable Israel to conquer it and to grant it a happy life there. It will also be recalled that the account of the solemnization of the covenant "at the foot of the mount" (on which Moses has been given the terms orally) comprises Exod 24:3-8, and that it is of a pronounced bilateral character. The human party to this pact is called "the people" in 24:3a, 3b, and 7. (In the received text, also in v. 8, but in Chapter IV, section d, I have given reasons for believing that here the original account had "the pillars.")

But the promise to the generation of the Exodus was conditional. Its conditional character is stressed explicitly in Lev 26, Jer. 11:3-5, and elsewhere (including Deut 28; for although Moses has all along been addressing those who had still been minors at the time of the covenant of Horeb, he has only relayed to them that which YHWH communicated to him alone on Mount Horeb after thundering out the "Ethical Decalogue" in the hearing of all the people; see Deut 5:18 ff., especially vv. 27 ff., plus Deut 6:1-3). And in any case, the conditional character of the promise to the generation of the Exodus became self-evident (as did that of the covenant with the House of David) when the calamities of the years 597 and 586 struck. What hope, therefore, could there be for the future? I

Deut 32:1 (along with the unmistakable identity of thought between Deut 32:1-3 and Isa 1:2) is too eloquent to be ignored.

have already observed that the far-fetched doctrine that "the nations" had — a good half-millennium before — witnessed YHWH's election of Israel as his people and still remembered it, and so would regard YHWH as discredited by Israel's loss of its national home until he repatriated it, would hardly have been thought up by Ezekiel and adopted by the first supplementer of Lev 26 if they had been able to fall back on an existing doctrine of an unconditional promise by YHWH to Abraham to give the land in perpetuity to his descendants. As a matter of fact, Ezekiel himself (Ezek 33:34–39) was aware (and disapproved) of the first groping toward such a doctrine among the Judites who were still left "on the soil of Israel," though he, pardonably, failed to realize what it would lead to. For we can see from Ezek 33:24 that the people in question were consoling themselves with the thought, "Abraham was but one man, yet he was granted possession of the land.[137] We are many; surely the land has been given as a possession to us."

A factor which encouraged the evolution of those gropings into a full-fledged doctrine of a promise (and that an unconditional one) by YHWH to Abraham to bestow the land in perpetuity upon his posterity, was the following coincidence. On the one hand, there was on old tradition, whose currency in preexilic times is vouched for by Hos 12:13[12] and Deut 26:5, that the Patriarchs were related to the Arameans; and on the other hand, just in the reign of Nabonidus, the last king of Babylon (556–539 B.C.E.), both Ur in southern Babylonia and Haran (Harran) which is situated so far north that it actually lies within present-day Turkey—the very two cities that are juxtaposed in Gen 11:31—attained great importance as centers of moon worship. The reason for this importance was that moon worship was favored by Nabonidus, a man of North Aramean stock whose mother was

---

[137] Even Gen 12:7, which J. Van Seters, *Abraham in History and Tradition* (see above, n. 133 end), p. 313, includes in the pre-Yahwistic core of the account of Abraham, has YHWH promise Abraham only to give "this land" to his descendents (though he does not say, "for all time"), and all passages agree that Abraham himself was only a resident alien in it. Besides, since v. 7b reports that Abram built an altar to YHWH "who had *appeared* (not "spoken") to him," v. 7aa may be an interpolation.

priestess of the moon-god Sin at Haran and who appointed his daughter priestess of the moon-god Nanna at Ur. Since, therefore, the Judite exiles lived not in northern but in southern Mesopotamia, one writer conceived the idea that Abraham had actually been born in Ur, and that the region of the northern Arameans from which he had set out for Canaan had been not his starting-point but a halfway station, which could even be ignored. Thus Abraham's migration from Babylonia to the land of Canaan prefigured a prospective return of his descendants to their homeland. And so Gen. 15:7ff (whose date is therefore exilic) relates that YHWH revealed himself to Abraham (in Canaan) as "YHWH, who brought you out from *Ur of Chaldea* to give you *this land* as a possession" (Gen 15:7), and that after nightfall, in the deep darkness, YHWH concluded with Abraham a solemn covenant to give "this land" to Abraham's descendants. The covenant was solemnized by the passage of YHWH, visible to a sleep-bound Abraham in a vision as "a pall of smoke[137a] and a flaming torch," passing between the halves of the heifer, the she-goat, and the ram that the Patriarch had previously bisected.

It is very suggestive, as Van Seters points out, that the nearest historical parallel to this ceremony is the one by which, according to Jer 34:18, the freemen of Jerusalem, practically on the eve of the extinction of the kingdom of Judah, covenanted to set free their Hebrew slaves. As for the term Ur of Chaldea, various attempts

---

[137a] The legitimate sense of *tannur* is in any case not 'fire pot' (RSV) or 'brazier' (NEB) but 'oven' (NJPS). However, the tradition behind the masoretic pointing of *'šn* as *'ašan* 'smoke' instead of *'ašen* 'smoking' (as in Exod 20:15; cf the plural *'ašenim,* Isa 7:4) presupposes for *tnwr* a sense similar to that of *tymrwt* (Joel 3:3, Song 3:10), with which cf *tmrtw* 'the smoke from it' (Bavli Berakot 43a, Ḥullin 112a). Our *tnwr* may therefore actually be a corruption of an original *tmr* or the like. The smoke is therefore to be regarded as produced by, or at any rate accessory to, the torch. The purpose of the passage of the covenanters through an analogous "covenant gate" in Jer 34:18–19 was no doubt to create a mystic bond of mutual obligation among them, like the dashing of blood from the same victims upon the two parties to the covenant of Exod 24:3–8. (See E. J. Bickerman "Couper une Alliance," in his *Studies in Jewish and Christian History* I. Leiden 1976, pp. 1 ff., especially pp. 1–15.) This motive is wanting in our Gen 15:7, since only one party assumes an obligation here (Gen 15:18–21); and the adaptation of the covenant gate ceremony to such a case is surely secondary.

have been made to identify the city with one of the similarly named northern ones and/or the region with the home of some assumed northern Chaldeans. But the only acceptable explanation today— what with the manner in which *Kaśdim* is employed elsewhere in Hebrew literature prior to Job 1:17 and the information available today about the Neo-Babylonian Empire (plus what was reported above about Nabonidus and his reign)—is the Chaldean nationality of Nabopolassar, who founded the Neo-Babylonian Empire in the year 626/5 B.C.E., and especially of his son and successor Nebuchadnezzar. For it was Nebuchadnezzar who, after expelling the Egyptians from all the territory between the Middle Euphrates in the north and the Egyptian border in the south, first subjugated and then, in two stages, liquidated the state of Judah and deported a large part of its population to Babylonia. That is why we find Hebrew writers — from II Ki 24:1; 25:5 ff. (through Jeremiah, Habakkuk, Ezekiel, and Isa 13:19) down to Isa 43:14; 47:1, 5; 48:14-20 — referring to Nebuchadnezzar's troops as *Kaśdim,* meaning Chaldeans, and to the region of southern Mesopotamia likewise as *Kaśdim,* meaning Chaldeans or Chaldea.

It is in the prophet cited almost at the end of the preceding paragraph, the seer of the 530's whom we call Second Isaiah (or Deutero-Isaiah), that we encounter what sounds like an echo of Gen 15:7 ff. Second Isaiah does not give up the saving-of-YHWH's-reputation motive devised by Ezekiel thirty years earlier (see Isa 43:25-28[138]; 48:9, 11), but he stresses more the idea of Gen 15 that YHWH summoned Abraham long ago "from the ends of the earth" (i.e. from faraway Ur of Chaldea) to be his friend.[139]

---

[138] With the footnote to Isa 43:28 in the Jewish Publication Society translation of The Prophets, Philadelphia 1978, emend *śare qodeś* to *śem qodśi* 'my holy name.'

[139] Isa 41:8-10 will gain much in clarity and force if—bearing in mind that "Israel . . . Jacob" in v. 8 means not the patriarch Jacob/Israel but the people of that name—one makes the relative clause in v. 9 refer *to Abraham,* reading *heḥzaqtiw* (["*of him*] whom I singled out"), *qratiw,* and *lo.* It is further advisable to translate the last three words in v. 9, "I have chosen you, I have never rejected you," so as to appreciate how likely the listening exiles were to take those words as addressed to them now as well as to Abraham centuries before.

Lyricist that he is, he does not refer to that place by name but by poetic circumlocutions; and, paralleling Jeremiah's appealing sentimentality in the passage referred to above (Jer 31:2[1] ff.), about the rehabilitation of the Israelians, our later rhapsodist substitutes for the making of a covenant with Abraham an outpouring of grace which is still inherited by Abraham's seed, Isa 41:8–13. It was surmised above that the consoling reflection of those of Ezekiel's contemporaries who had remained behind in Judah (to the effect that after all Abraham had "possessed" the land though he was only one man) is to be regarded as the first groping toward a doctrine of YHWH's having made to Abraham a promise of the land which was still valid. As if to confirm that surmise, there appears in Isa 51:1–4 another piece of reasoning from the fact that Abraham was only one man. However, the point that Second Isaiah makes is different from that of Ezekiel's contemporaries, and his hopes are pitched much higher. If, he argues, YHWH was able to bless and increase Abraham who, at the time of his election, was only one man, what doubt can there be about his ability to rehabilitate Zion? (Zion here means all of Judah, and perhaps also the territory of the former kingdom of Israel which has been occupied by aliens, cf. Isa 54:3.)

We have already seen that the doctrine of the promise to Abraham was adopted by P—who even extended the covenanted, or sworn, promise to all three of the Patriarchs (so already Gen. 17:7–8, 19, 35:12)—and that it gave rise to interpolations elsewhere. The case of Exod 32:13 is clear. Not only does it break the connection between vv. 12 and 14, but it is irrelevant in view of v. 10b, since the great nation that YHWH there proposes to make of Moses would also come under the heading of "posterity of Abraham, Isaac, and Jacob." Likewise an interpolation is Exod 33:1b, as are (this was pointed out in Chapter IV b) the words "to your fathers" in Exod 13:1b and "to you and your fathers" in Exod 13:11.

As for Deuteronomy, Van Seters[140] distinguishes two kinds of

---

[140] 'Confessional reformulation,' pp. 451–2.

interpolation. There is first of all the case of Deut 9:27, which is of course intrusive just as we have seen Exod 32:13 to be. To this observation of Van Seters I would add that the entire paragraph Deut 9:25–29 (the correct rendering of whose initial half-verse is "When I lay prostrate those 40 days and 40 nights," as was pointed out in Chapter VIII) is a secondary elaboration of Deut 9:18 inspired by Exod 32:11–13 (cf. the relative clause at the end of Deut 9:29 with Exod 32:11 from "Your people" to the end); and it takes along the appeal of Exod 32:13—which is itself secondary—to remember the Patriarchs, but omits to include what is explicit in Exod 32:13, namely, that to those Patriarchs YHWH swore to give the land to their descendants. This is an example of the sort of thing that Van Seters himself has characterized as a "blind motif."[140]

The other mentions of YHWH's promises to, or election of, "your fathers" in Deuteronomy are a more complex problem. Van Seters tries to solve it[141] by noting that in Deut 1:8; 6:10; 9:5; 29:12; 30:20 the names of the three Patriarchs are not introduced directly, as in 34:4, "which is commonly regarded as JE," and in Exod 32:13; 33:1; Num 32:11, but follow "your fathers" in apposition; so that if what follows "your fathers" is removed as an interpolation, "your fathers" can mean the generation of the Exodus. However, while this works more or less well with many of the occurrences of "your fathers" in Deuteronomy, provided one adds a certain explanation, it does not even then work with all of them. The explanation I have in mind is this. It was during the year of the Exodus that there occurred the celebrated incident of the scouts who reconnoitered the Promised Land and brought back a discouraging report which precipitated a loss of nerve among the people. As punishment for this lack of faith, YHWH decreed that every person who was at that time twenty years old or more should perish before the others could enter the land. Now, in the fortieth year of the desert wanderings, when Moses addressed the people in the land of Moab, the only persons still left who had not been

---

[141] *Abraham in History and Tradition*, pp. 163, 180, 183, 188.

minors at the time of the decree were Caleb — who had been spared to enter the land as a reward for stoutheartedly maintaining, against the other scouts (who in the E-D tradition remain anonymous), that the land definitely could be conquered — and Moses, who had been told that he would die shortly before the people crossed the Jordan under the leadership of Joshua. For the latter is regarded in the E-D tradition as not having yet attained his majority in the year of the Exodus (cf. "a youth," Exod 33:11). Accordingly, the adults in the congregation addressed by Moses in the fortieth year were all (with the exception of Caleb) between the ages of twenty and fifty-eight. Thirty-nine years earlier, therefore, enough of them had been in their teens to warrant (if the author kept such a careful check on the arithmetic) Moses' appealing to them as having witnessed with their own eyes and heard with their own ears the prodigies of the plagues in Egypt, the revelation at Horeb, etc. (Deut 4:9-18, 33-34; 5:3-4, 19; 10:21; 11:2-8); but since even these members of his audience had not attained their majority at that time, the recipients of the promise of the land had necessarily been "your fathers," the very ones who had expired during the intervening thirty-nine years. That would justify the references to "your fathers" in Deut 6:10 (here only if one regards the apposition of the names of the Patriarchs as an interpolation with Van Seters), 18, 23; 7:8, 12; 8:1, 18, etc. But in Deut 1:8, where Moses is reporting that which "our God YHWH said to us at Horeb" (ibid. v. 6), i.e. in the year of the Exodus, even taking out "to Abraham, Isaac, and Jacob" leaves "to your fathers" incorrect on the hypothesis that those addressed had but recently received the promise themselves. Indeed, the words "which YHWH swore" (instead of "which I swore") in a speech of YHWH himself shows that the author was here off guard; and, since this is part of the *later* introduction to Deuteronomy (1:1—4:43), it is just as well, in this case, not to cancel the names of the Patriarchs but to assume that this stratum of Deuteronomy postdates the exilic-postexilic "confessional reformulation." I take the same view of the fathers-plus-apposition formula in 29:12 and

30:20, since these verses pertain to the *later* conclusion of Deuteronomy, Deut 28:69—30:20. Evidently, the amount of post-722 augmentation and manipulation to which the late-Israelian core of Deuteronomy was subjected after its migration to Judah and after the fall of the latter is not to be minimized.[142]

Also of relevance here is that aspect of M. Haran's book of 1978[143] which is named at the end of its subtitle: "the historical setting of the Priestly School." According to Haran, the School arose in the age of Hezekiah, and it was not Proto-Deuteronomy but the earliest stratum of the Priestly Code that inspired the reformation of Hezekiah which is reported in II Ki 18:4—even though, according to Haran, all the strata of the PC remained esoteric until they were made authoritative by Ezra. Against this bold theory may be urged all the abundant evidence to the contrary that is included in the body of the present work—especially Chapters III–VII—as also in the foregoing pages of this Postscript. But one point that is made in Chapter III is worth enlarging upon here. Hezekiah's measures, according to the verse in II Kings which has just been cited (II Ki 18:4), included the cutting down *(krt)* of the cult post *('ašera),* and it is hard to see how that can be anything but a response to the prohibition of Deut 16:21 against the planting *(nṭ')* of such an object next to the altar of YHWH. For within the Pentateuch the word *'ašera* only occurs again in Deut 12:3 (as object of

---

[142] A particularly disturbing interpolation is Deut 10:6–7. It is not only unconnected with what precedes it and conspicuous by its third person "the Israelites," instead of the first person "we" or the second person (plural) "you" that are normal in this book because it is cast in the form of an address by Moses to the Israelites. What is even more significant is that it reports that Aaron died and was succeeded in the priesthood by his son Eleazar, whereas Deuteronomy proper confers the priesthood on the undifferentiated Levites, e.g. immediately after this interpolation, in 10:8. It is only P which, hardly before the Persian period, limits the priesthood to a caste said to be descended from Aaron and which, from Exod 6:20 on, makes Aaron not merely a fellow Levite but a full brother of Moses and, in Num 26:59, explicitly adds Miriam to his siblings. There is no reason to believe that Deut 9:20 and 24:9 presuppose those late developments; for the older—probably historically correct—tradition, see above n. 103.

[143] M. Haran, *Temples and Temple Service in Ancient Israel: An Inquiry into the Character of Cult Phenomena and the Historical Setting of the Priestly School,* Oxford 1978.

śrp 'to burn'), in Deut 7:5 as object of *gd'* 'to cut down,' and in Exod 34:13—which we have seen in Chapter VI is adapted from Deut 7:5—as object of the other Hebrew word for 'to cut down,' the very *krt* of II Ki 18:4! P, on the other hand, exhibits not a single instance of *'ašera* or of any other expression that might conceivably mean the same thing.[144]

---

[144] The edge of this argument cannot be blunted with the observation that, for that matter, neither does *bama/bamot* occur in D, whereas at least H employs it in Lev 26:30. For here the context speaks of shrines of *gillulim,* or fetishes, whereas the need for a term for local, though (as in most passages in Kings) not necessarily idolatrous, shrines only arose when the Deuteronomic doctrine that sacrifices are only permissible at the one site "that your God YHWH will choose" was applied in practice. (In Mi 3:12, bamot yá'ar means 'a wooded height' [so rightly RSV], not 'a woodland shrine' [so erroneously NJPS], and in Mi 1:5b bamot is obviously to be corrected to *hattot* [or *hattat*] in the light of the Septuagint and of v. 5a.) The Deuteronomic reformation of Josiah, which, unlike that of Hezekiah, proved definitive, brought in its wake still further refinements of terminology. Thus *hehêti,* which in Deut 24:4 is applied to the *defilement of the land* by revolting practices, is specialized in Kings to denote the *bringing of guilt* by a ruler *on his subjects* through illegitimate (though not necessarily apostatizing) cultic practices, whereas for the pollution of the land Jeremiah (Jer 2:7; 3:1,2) employs *tm'* and *hnp,* as does also P (Num 35:33–34).

ADDENDA

To p. 43 middle. For an excellent discussion of *psḥ,* see *E.S. Loewenstamm,* The Tradition of the Exodus in its Development (English title of the Hebrew work), Jerusalem 1965, pp. 84 ff.

To ch. VII and p. 85 n. 105. Other late elements in P are cited by *B.A. Levine,* Interpreter's Dictionary of the Bible, Supplementary Volume 685b. For example, Levine recalls the proper name *Parnak* (Num 34:25), which has already been identified, and not unreasonably, with the Persian name *Pharnaces,* and the common noun *dégel* 'military unit' (Num 2 and 10), which the Bible never has any other occasion to employ in connection with any force, Hebrew or otherwise, but which occurs frequently as *dgl* in the fifth century Aramaic papyri from Elephantine and occasionally in the fourth century Aramaic ostraca fragments from Arad. It seems that Levine learned about the occurrence of *dgl* at Arad privately from Aharoni (Interpreter's Dictionary ibid. p. 633a) and that that is the basis for his quotation of the phrase *ldgl 'bdḥy* (which would leave open the possibility that the commander of the unit was a Jew). However, the definitive publication of the Arad inscriptions, which has meanwhile become available (see above, p. 68 n. 83) and in which all the Aramaic ostraca fragments on which any writing is still legible are edited with photographs and interpreted by Yosef Naveh, reveals that the word *dgl* actually occurs in two of the ostraca (nos. 12 and 18) and that in the one in which the name of the commander is preserved it is not *'bdḥy* but *'bdnny.* Naveh rightly connects the element *nny* with the name of the Babylonian deity ("Goddess"—so, rightly, Naveh) Nanna (see above, p. 110). Thus, just as in fifth century Elephantine Jews served in *dgln* com-

117

manded by men with Persian or Akkadian Babylonian names, so in fourth century Arad we find them serving under a man with an Aramaic Babylonian name. The term *dgl* is therefore unlikely to have been introduced into Imperial Aramaic by Jews, and Levine's hypothesis that *dgl* in Num 2 and 10 is of Imperial Aramaic origin is not unreasonable. For the cognate material adduced by Baumgartner (see above, p. 3 n. 3) includes Arabic *dajjālat* and Tigré *dagal,* both of which denote a considerable body of men.

To p. 95. On the Joseph story, see *D.A. Redford,* A Study of the Biblical Story of Joseph (VT Supplement 20), Leiden 1970, and add especially that it is now recognized that *ṭ'n* 'to load,' Gen 45:17 does *not* occur in Ugaritic and is borrowed from post-700 B.C.E. Aramaic (its genuine Hebrew etymon being *ṣ'n,* Isa 33:20). The story also contains other Aramaisms.

To pp. 46 f. n. 62   The last eight lines of n. 62 call attention to two features of the passage Deut. 5:6–18 which call for comment. 1. According to Deut 10:1–4 (whence also 4:24), the writing on the tablets recorded "the Ten Words (or Articles)" which YHWH proclaimed to the Israelites assembled at Horeb. 2. According to Deut 5:3–3, that address constituted a *covenant* between YHWH and Israel; and in line with this characterization of the tablets' content, the ark in which they were deposited is referred to in Deut 10:5, 8 as "the Ark of YHWH's Covenant," while Deut 26:69 (in introducing the covenant entered into in the land of Moab) refers back to "the *covenant* that [YHWH] made with them at Horeb."

Now, the covenants of YHWH are of two types: in one (which bears a certain resemblance to the covenant by which Jonathan undertook to be David's "patron," I Sam 18:3–4), only YHWH assumes an obligation; in the other, both YHWH and the human party assume obligations. (There are also cases in which *brit* is rather an imposed obligation than an agreed one, and where it might be better to render it by *order* than by covenant; e.g. Isa 24:5; Hos 6:6; 5:1.) Of the several YHWH-covenants of the first type the most interesting are, perhaps: 1. the covenant with

Noah's family and every other form of (non-aquatic) life that had
survived the Flood, whereby God bound himself never again to
bring upon the earth a flood of universal extermination (Gen 9:8
ff.); 2. the covenant with Abram to bestow upon his descendants
a country stretching from Egypt to the Euphrates (Gen 15:9 ff.);
3. a priestly variant of the preceding, according to which God
assumed a similar obligation toward all three of the Patriarchs,
first Abraham and Isaac (Gen 17:18, 19) and then Jacob (Gen
35:9–12), these covenants being recalled in the P strand Exod
1:1–5, 7, 13–14; 2:23 (beginning with "the Israelites groaned on
account of this labor")–25; 6:3–8.

YHWH-covenants of the second type—two-way covenants—
have already been dealt with on pp. 45 ff. and 62 ff. and the above-
cited reference (in Deut 28:69) to the covenant of Horeb (i.e. that
of 5:6–18) itself introduces a covenant in which YHWH (in 29:12)
as well as Israel assumes an obligation. Where, then, in Deut
5:6–18[21] is the obligation assumed by YHWH? Intimately connected with this problem is that of the identification of the individual Ten Words.

G. Beer, *Exodus* (= Handbuch zum Alten Testament, Erste
Reihe 3), 1939, p. 99, conveniently describes the three manners of
dividing the Decalogue and the authors and sects that subscribe to
them; cf. in English M.D. Koster, VT 30 (1980), p. 469. All three
methods, I find, commit the error of dividing the version in Exod
20 and that in Deut 5 in the identical manner, so that none of them
can approach critical correctness in more than one version. Thus,
Beer's System II, that of "Augustin, die römischen Katholiken,
Luther und die Lutheraner," is almost perfectly satisfactory when
applied to Deut. 5. For that Deut 5:18a and 18b[21a and 21b] are
two distinct prohibitions is indubitably the text's own intention.
This is definitely not the case in Exod 20:14[17]. Here the a-verse,
"You shall not covet your fellow man's *báyit,*" can only mean, "You
shall not covet your fellow man's *household,*" of which the b-verse,
which names the wife as well as the male or female slave, etc., can
only be an explication. Exod 20:14[17] would therefore seem to be

a more primitive formulation which Deut 5:18[21] deliberately modified. Here it is the a-verse that forbids the coveting of one's fellow man's wife; while the b-verse is reserved for items of his property, including his *land* (*śade*), which is altogehter wanting in Exod 20:14[17], as well as his *báyit,* which must here mean not household but *house.* In the circumstances, it is hard to escape the conclusion that the use of two different verbs in the two halves of v. 18[21] *(lo taḥmod* and *lo tit'awwe)* is deliberate (contrast the situation in Exod 20:14[17], where the b-verse merely repeats the *lo taḥmod* of the a-verse) and is intended to stress the desire of the reformulator to have the two halves of Deut 5:18[21] counted as two separate "words" of the total of ten. In the case of Deut 5:18[21], therefore, the only error in Beer's System II is that it counts the introductory sentence, "I YHWH am your God who delivered you from a state of bondage (so no doubt rightly Ehrlich on Exod 20:2) in Egypt," as part of the first commandment. For in the intention of D, Deut 5:6 is rather *YHWH's commitment* under the covenant of Horeb; cf. Ezek 20:5 (see above, p. 105, for a translation), also Num 15:41, and note I Sam 12:22: "For since YHWH undertook to make you his people, he will, for the sake of his great name, never forsake his people."

Thus the Horeb covenant of Deut 5 comprises one commitment of YHWH and ten precepts for Israel, just like the covenants discussed on pp. 45 ff. and 62 ff. But whereas the two latter are strictly cultic decalogues, the decalogue of (Exod 20:2–14[17]//) Deut 5:6–18[21] may not unfittingly be distinguished from them by Wellhausen's term "the Ethical Decalogue."

From my observations on pp. 45 ff. and in Chapter VI, it follows that Exod 20:2–14[17], unlike Deut 5:6–18[21], is nowhere actually described as either a decalogue or a covenant. If therefore it is patient of interpretation as either the one or the other (or as both), it does not strictly follow that it is intended as either; but the possibilities deserve to be studied. Now, to be sure, the Exodus version, in contrast to the Deuteronomy one, resists any attempt to fit it into Beer's System II, precisely because, as we have seen, Exod

20:14[17] constitutes not two commandments but one. All the more tempting as an analysis of Exod 20:2–14[17] is Beer's System I—that of "Philo, Josephus, the primitive Church, and Reformed, Socinian, and Greek Catholic" Christians—which counts only one commandment against coveting but on the other hand understands the prohibition of the making and worshiping of images (Exod 20:4–7 [//Deut 5:8–10]) as an independent commandment. Apply this to Exod 20:2–14[17], and it is only necessary to detach v. 2 from the first commandment and treat it (in the same manner as we did Deut 5:6 in our modification of System II as applied to Deut 5:6–18[21]) as YHWH's undertaking under the covenant. But one may hesitate to conclude that that is how Exod 20:2–14[17] was intended to be understood, in view of the fact that the formulator of Deut 5:8–18[21], who as we have seen probably had Exod 20:2–14[17] as his model, either was not aware that in his model the prohibition against images was an independent commandment or else chose to disregard that feature of it when he treated the said prohibition as merely a part of the prohibition of the worship of other gods.

The only traditional system that recognizes the independent character of the introductory declaration, "I YHWH am your God etc.," is Beer's System III, the normative Jewish one. It does not, however, in either of the two versions of the Ethical Decalogue regard this declaration (as I have done in the case of the Deuteronomy version) as a self-obligation of God; rather, it regards it as (in both versions) a commandment equivalent to "You must acknowledge that I . . . am your God who delivered you etc."—Ehrlich on Exod 20:2 endeavors to avoid this interpretation of the verse by arguing that the traditional Jewish name of the Decalogue is not the Ten Commandments but the Ten Words (biblical *dbarim,* postbiblical *dibbrot* [the latter form being the plural of the noun *dibber* 'word of God,' which occurs already in Jeremiah 5:13 and is common in scientifically edited rabbinic texts—see for example the reading and interpretation of the first few lines of Mekilta in the Horovitz-Rabin edition, which follows the readings of the two earliest printings (Constantinople 1515, Venice 1545) and the interpretation of Middot Soferim]). However, Prof. David Weiss Halivni calls my attention to Bavli Makkot 23b bottom-24a top, where *'Anoki* (Exod 20:2// Deut 5:6), no less than *Lo yihye lka* (Exod 20:3–7//Deut 5:7–10), is unmistakably counted as one of the total of 613 commandments (*miṣwot*) that the Torah is there assumed to contain.—For the normative Jewish identification of the Ten Words, see Mekilta Baḥódesh VIII, ed. Horovitz-Rabin pp. 233–5; ed. Lauterbach (with English translation), vol. II, pp. 262–4.

To pp. 67 ff.:   Further Arguments for a Manassean Dating of the Introduction of the Numbered-Months Calendar

That Lev 23:4-44 and Num 26:16—29:33 postdate Deut 16:1 ff. and Exod 34:10-27, follows logically, we have seen, from the varying provisions of these pericopes for (a) the apotropaic ("Passover") sacrifice and the season of unleavened bread, (b) the grain harvest, and (c) the Pilgrimage of Ingathering/Booths; in other words, the late dating of the said blocks of Leviticus and Numbers does not depend on a late dating of what I have named the numbered-months calendar. However, if the latter can be proved to have been adopted in the reign of Manasseh, the case for a late dating of parts, at least, of H and P will appear even stronger; besides, a demonstration of the Manassean origin of the numbered-months calendar is worthwhile for its own sake.

My view that Israel's original calendar had a fall startingpoint agrees with that of B.S. Childs in *The Book of Exodus, A Critical Theological Commentary,* Philadelphia 1974, and of M. Noth in his commentaries on Exodus, Leviticus, and Numbers (English translations of which are included, like Child's work, in The Old Testament Library). These writers cite, as I have, the Gezer Calendar and Exod 23:16b; 34:22b. I trust, however, that my distinction between *bṣet haṣṣana* 'at the *beginning* of the year' in pre-Deuteronomic Exod 23:10b and *tqupat haṣṣana* 'the end of the year' in para-Deuteronomic Exod 34:22b will commend itself to such as follow my reasoning carefully. Worthy of commendation is, in addition,

Noth's observation in his commentaries on Leviticus and Numbers that the secondary character of the numbered-months calendar with its spring startingpoint is betrayed by Lev 23:24 and Num 29:1, inasmuch as these verses date the day of *tru'a* 'rousing calls (of the ram's horn),' i.e. *New Year's* Day, on the first day of the *seventh* month, and by Lev 25:9, inasmuch as this verse requires that *the year of release,* or jubilee, *be ushered in* throughout the nation by blarings of rams' horns on the tenth day of, again, the *seventh* month. I take the liberty of adding the observation that, although the prooftexts cited in Mekilta Bo I (ed. Horovitz-Rabin p. 7) are Deut 31:4, Exod 23:16b, and Exod 34:22b, it was surely primarily because of Noth's Leviticus and Numbers passages that Judaism in tannaitic times began to call the first day of just the "seventh" month *roš haššanna* 'the beginning of the year' and to treat it accordingly, thus reverting, in effect, to the ante-Manassean "fall opening" calendar. This was made easier by the fact that the ordinal numerals had meanwhile, during the Persian period, been superseded by the Aramaic forms of the corresponding Babylonian month-names—in this particular case, the appellation "the seventh month" by "(the month of) Tishri." As it happens, this name, which is descriptive, is not inappropriate for the month in its new, Jewish, position, since its Akkadian form *Tašrît* means 'beginning.' To be sure, in its original application—to the Assyro-Babylonian seventh month—it denoted not the beginning of the year but the beginning of *the winter half* of the year. For (as I am informed by Prof. Moshe Held of Columbia University) the Akkadian *ebūru* 'harvest, summer' and *kuṣṣu* 'winter' are juxtaposed as comprising between them the whole year just like the corresponding Hebrew *qáyiṣ* and *ḥórep* (Zech 14:8b; Ps 74:17) or the denominative verbs *qyṣ* 'to summer' and *ḥrp* 'to winter' (Isa 18:6b), no doubt because a basic division of the year into only two seasons was suggested to both of these speech communities by the subtropical climate they lived in. Still, the only case in which the Jewish shift of the year's beginning from Nisan to Tishri resulted in a real incongruity (though tannaitic Jewry could not have been aware of it) was in the new position of Marḥeshwan, originally the eighth month, as second. For the Akkadian original of *Marḥeshwan—Araḥsaman* (pronounced Araḥsawan)—means precisely 'eighth month.' [A helpful analogy is the following. At Rome the official beginning of the year was once the fifteenth of March, but in the year 153 B.C.E. it was changed to the first of January; and that was how our *September* ("no. 7"), *October* ("no. 8"), *November* ("no. 9"), and *December* ("no. 10") came to be the misnomers they are.]

My dating of the adoption of the Mesopotamian "spring opening" calendar in the reign of Manasseh (698–642) is probably higher than that of Noth and most others who, like me, defend a late dating of the priestly literature (or much of it). Yet, since H. Tadmor, in his valuable article on chronology in *Enṣiqlopedia Miqra'it* IV, cols. 245 ff., observes (col. 268 bottom) that the postdating of the reigns from that of Amon on "may be due to the growth of Assyrian influence on Judah under Assyrian suzerainty in the reign of Manasseh," what would be more natural than the adoption of the Assyro-Babylonian calendar in the same period from the same cause? Tadmor (col. 264) states that the earliest datings of events by the numbered-months spring-to-spring calendar date from the time of Jeremiah. I hesitate to descend that low for the adoption of the calendar in question for the following reason: Jer 34:13–14 is based on Deut 15:12, which in turn (see above p. 100) makes use of Lev 25 (as well as of Exod 21); and Lev 25:9 contains the words "in the seventh month, on the tenth day of the month," which there are hardly solid reasons for regarding as a gloss. In contrast, the long span of years from the accession of Manasseh (698) to the promulgation of Proto-Deuteronomy (with some post-Hezekian expansions) in the 18th year of Josiah (622) is ample for accommodating the adoption of the numbered-months calendar (identical, apart from the names of the months, with the Assyro-Babylonian one) as well as the composition of Lev 25 and Deut 15. (For Deut 15, one could even descend a little below 622 B.C.E. if necessary.) [The legislation in Lev 25 reflects a distressing frequency of impoverishment whose victims are compelled to sell their lands and sometimes themselves. I am therefore tempted to conjecture that the very same conditions may have impelled some Judites to migrate to Egypt, perhaps at first (in part) as mercenaries of Manasseh and his Assyrian suzerains, perhaps becoming mercenaries of native Egyptian princes, and in any case eventually becoming (in the persons of the well-known Judite military colonists on Elephantine) mercenaries of the Persian king.—N.B. Note the wording at the end of the last sentence but one: *"to sell* their lands and sometimes *themselves."* Against W. Baumgartner et al., *Hebräisches und aramäisches Lexikon zum Alten Testament,* Dritte Auflage (1974), p. 551a, the force of the nifals of *mkr* in Lev 25:39, 42; Deut 15:12; Jer 34:14 must be understood not as passive but as reflexive. NJPS bungles Deut 15:12, but it hits the nail on the head ('to give oneself over') in Lev 25:39, 42, and at least offers the truth as an alternative (or "who sells himself") in a footnote to Jer 34:14.]

But was, perhaps, some sort of calendar with a spring opening employed by a significant segment of the Israelite people even before Manasseh? Tadmor believes that there are data which show that the startingpoint of a regnal year was not the same in Israel as in Judah, and therefore assumes that the situation that is attested for Judah in its latest decades had obtained there all along except that we don't know by what names the months had been designated prior to the days of Jeremiah (or, he might say in light of the foregoing, Manasseh), whereas in the kingdom of Israel a fall startingpoint had been observed. The data from which he infers the existence of a gap between the limits of the year in the two kingdoms are (col. 267) that whereas Zechariah is said to have succeeded his father as king of Israel in the 38th year of Uzziah of Judah and to have reigned only six months in all, both Zechariah's successor Shallum and Shallum's successor Menahem are said to have acceded to the kingship in Uzziah's 39th year (II Ki 15:8, 13, 17). But these data can be reconciled with a hypothesis that regnal years ran from fall to fall at both royal courts, if it is surmised that the assassination of Zechariah took place either in the last month of Uzziah's 38th year or in (or just after) the first month of his 39th. In the former case, the editor in question will have figured that it would be absurd to count part of the year of Zechariah's accession, just because of the fraction of a month by which his death preceded the end of it, to the reign of that king-for-a-month Shallum; in the latter case, he will have decided that it was more practical to ignore the month (or less) that Zechariah lingered on into the following calendar year, since the reign of the hapless last monarch of the line of Jehu in fact lasted only half a year. For such treatments of fractional months or years by the compiler(s), see Tadmor, cols. 268 bottom-269 top, 267 ll. 7 ff. and 287 ll. 18 ff. The possibility of still another omission of some odd month is contemplated in col. 297 ll. 14–13 from below. Tadmor also cites an example of something similar from Assyrian history (col. 269 top): because on the day of his accession only one month and 12 days of the current calendar year had elapsed, Tiglathpileser deviated from the Assyrian postdating practice and counted that year instead of the following one as his first regnal year.

After all the foregoing circumstantial evidence, lexicographical confirmation of the priority of the fall-opening calendar in Israel is not necessary, but some happens to be available. We have already encountered the Hebrew word *ḥórep* 'winter.' That its root meaning is "earliness," so that it reflects a calendar like the Gezer one, in which the winter half of the year precedes the summer half, was first suggested to me by *bime ḥorpi,* Job 29:4, which Rashi interprets to mean 'in my earlier days' in light of the Babylonian Aramaic *ḥrpy w'ply* 'coming earlier in some years and later in others' (with reference to the seasons of grape-treading and olivepressing), Nidda 65b. (*Ḥrpy . . . 'ply* occurs again in Ta'ănit 3a, where it refers to clouds of the earlier and later parts of the winter half-year.) Rashi's exegesis of Job 29:4 has not won universal acceptance; but even if it should be necessary to dispense with it, a cast-iron demonstration that *ḥórep* 'winter' means eymologically what I claim it does and reflects the kind of calendar I claim it does, is possible with Akkadological material for which I am again indebted to Prof. Moshe Held. In Akkadian, not only are a verb *ḫarāpu* 'to be, or to do something, early' and an adjective *ḫarpu* 'early' (with the corresponding adverb *ḫarpis*) well attested, but there is a noun *ḫarpū* (lit. "the earlies"—plurale tantum), a dialectal synonym of the *ebūru* '(harvest) summer' we encountered above. Obviously, the so derived *ḫarpū* 'summer' reflects the Mesopotamian calendar with its spring startingpoint. Add this result to all the arguments I have already adduced for the character of the original Israelite calendar, and virtually no room is left for doubts but the Hebrew *ḥôrep* 'winter' likewise means etymologically "earliness" and for its part reflects the ante-Manassean calendar of all Israel with its autumn startingpoint.

Bibliographical Abbreviations

ANET	Ancient Near Eastern Texts Relating to the Old Testament, Third Edition with Supplement, Princeton 1969.
BASOR	Bulletin of the American Schools of Oriental Research
HTR	Harvard Theological Review
IEJ	Israel Exploration Journal
JBL	Journal of Biblical Literature
JSS	Journal of Semitic Studies
NEB	New English Bible
NJPS	The new Bible translation of The Jewish Publication Society of America
PAAJR	Proceedings of the American Academy for Jewish Research
RSV	Revised Standard Version
VT	Vetus Testamentum

Index of Authors*

*Numbers refer to pages; notes not distinguished from text.

131

INDEX OF BIBLE PASSAGES

132

Deuteronomy

*The verse numbers are those of the printed Hebrew Bible, in which most superscriptions count as separate verses.